# HOW TO
# LAND A JUMBO JET

# HOW TO
# LAND A
# JUMBO
# JET

## A Visual Exploration of Travel Facts, Figures and Ephemera

**EDITED BY NIGEL HOLMES**

# CONTENTS

# INTRODUCTION

So what is an information graphic – an infographic – anyway?

It's a term that's much younger than the thing it describes. (A quick search suggests that it came into general usage in the 1970s.)

But information graphics themselves have been around for much longer – around 32,000 years, in fact.

That's when the first known drawings were made, in the Chauvet Cave in France. Although there's some argument about their meaning, it is now generally agreed that the purpose of the paintings was to deliver information and to teach, rather than to be purely art for art's sake. They were the first information graphics.

They were beautiful, too. More than 32,000 years later, strict academic observers of today's information design sometimes forget this attribute, as they argue against anything that might excite the reader in the way of pictorial elements, or color, or fun. These critics come from a school of thought that excludes everything except the facts, and that often results in clinical graphics which are undeniably proper and neat, but are easily forgotten.

In the world of infographics there is room and reason for many types, and in here you'll find good examples of the different strands of current work in this fast developing field – some are largely pictorial, others are minimal and analytical. Some are colorful, others use a very restricted palette, or no color at all. And as you'd expect from a book that's about different aspects of travel, there are all sorts of exciting graphic adventures waiting for you.

I raise a glass to toast all the designers for their hard work, and I hope you, dear reader, enjoy the result, learn something new, and set off on even happier journeys!

Nigel Holmes

# How to Land a Jumbo Jet

*"These things almost land themselves, don't they?"*
—Kurt Russell to Halle Berry in *Executive Decision*, 1996

Russell wasn't exactly right in that movie, but big jets do have an autopilot (and some airlines insist that their planes make an autoland every 30 days).

**1** The first thing to do is to level the plane. If it's descending or climbing, this probably means that the autopilot is off. Look at the **attitude indicator,** and pull on the **yoke** (the plane's steering wheel) to raise the nose and correct the descent (or push the yoke to lower the nose and correct a climb).

**2** Turn on the **autopilot** (three switches: A, B, C) and the **autobrake selector**.

**3** Call for help. Say "Mayday"* three times into the **pilot's headset.** Add the flight number. You'll be answered by an airport flight controller. Listen carefully. The flight controller will know the layout of the plane's controls and will help you find the necessary buttons and switches.

*Mayday comes from the French *m'aider,* meaning help me. It originated in 1923.

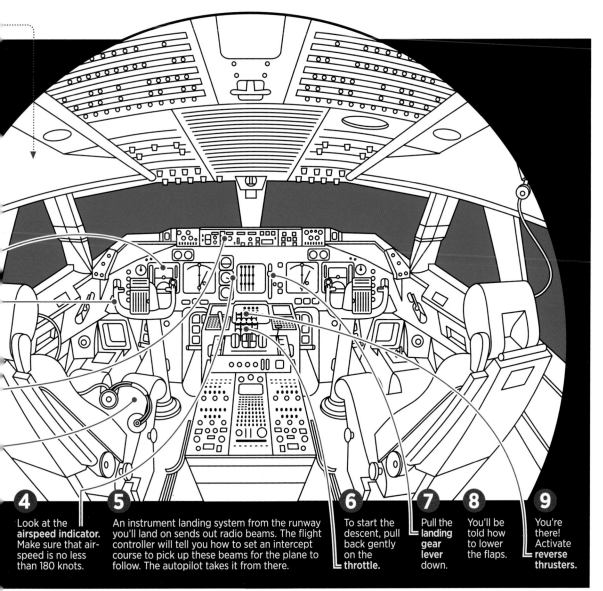

**4** Look at the **airspeed indicator.** Make sure that airspeed is no less than 180 knots.

**5** An instrument landing system from the runway you'll land on sends out radio beams. The flight controller will tell you how to set an intercept course to pick up these beams for the plane to follow. The autopilot takes it from there.

**6** To start the descent, pull back gently on the **throttle.**

**7** Pull the **landing gear lever** down.

**8** You'll be told how to lower the flaps.

**9** You're there! Activate **reverse thrusters.**

Artist's disclaimer: this is a simplified overview of the complicated landing procedure. If I were you, I wouldn't volunteer! (And be careful what you eat in a plane.)

# PLACES **TO GO NUDE!**

**TAKE A NAKATION!** A nakation is a clothing optional vacation. People who take a nakation visit sites that support the nudist lifestyle, sites that offer clothing optional facilities for guests who wish to take advantage of them.

**FREE!**

**1** WORLD NAKED BIKE RIDE

**AUSTRALIA, BRAZIL, DENMARK etc**

Celebrated in 70 cities and 20 countries around the world, people hop on their bikes naked to celebrate cycling and the naked body!

**2** ENGLISCHER GARTEN

**MUNICH, GERMANY**

It is one of Europe's biggest city parks covering nearly 4 sq km. Nude sunbathing is permitted within the Schönfeldwiese part of the park.

**3** WORLD BODY PAINTING FESTIV

**PÖRTSCHACH AM WÖRTHERSEE, AUSTRIA**

Europe's biggest and most colourful art event of its kind. Around 30,000 visitors, artists, photographers and musicians from more than 40 nations.

**NOT FREE!**

**10** NAKED SPA TREATMENTS

**AYANA RESORT & SPA, BALI**

Rejuvenate your senses with the resort's quintessential healing and indulgent therapies.

**9** NAKED HOT SPRINGS

**OOEDO-ONSEN-MONOGATARI, TOKYO, JAPAN**

Tourists are able to strip off and soak in mineral-rich natural hot springs in the traditional Japanese way.

**8** KOTIHARJUN SAUNA

**KALLIO, HELSINKI, FINLAND**

The only remaining wood-burning sauna in the world. Dating back to 1928, this is a truly Finnish experience. You can also get a scrub-down and massage.

# Q: WOULD YOU RIDE ON A NUDIST AIRLINE (IF THERE'S ONE)?

Total (male and female)

79%

21%

- YES! YES! YES!
- GROSS

**48%** of Americans would be willing to go nude at a beach. The not-too-serious poll of **22,091** Americans was conducted by TripAdvisor, an online travel community.

**38%** of all Canadians would or have walked around the house nude.

## ETIQUETTE / TIPS WHEN VISITING NUDE BEACHES

### *4* NAKED CITY

CAP D'AGDE, FRANCE

People going about their business in the buff. The entire town is clothing-optional and it is known as the world's capital of naturism.

### *5* HAULOVER BEACH

MIAMI, FLORIDA, USA

This nude beach near Miami is one of the few "legal" nude beaches in the United States. It is ideal for surfing, swimming and sunbathing.

1. **DO NOT STARE**
2. **BE POLITE TO EVERYONE**
3. **ALWAYS ASK FOR PERMISSION BEFORE TAKING A PICTURE**
4. **OPEN SEXUAL BEHAVIOR IS NOT ALLOWED.**
5. **BE SURE TO USE SUNSCREEN!**

### *7* BURNING MAN

BLACK ROCK DESERT, NEVADA, USA

An annual cultural festival where partakers are encouraged to express themselves in a number of ways through various art forms and projects.

### *6* NAKED CRUISE

SPLIT, CROATIA

Organised by cruising company eWaterways, the 8-day cruise offers bold holidaymakers a chance to strip off along the stunning Dalmatian Coast.

**DID YOU KNOW THERE IS AN IPHONE APPLICATION THAT TELLS YOU WHERE TO GET NAKED**

**SOURCES**

http://www.bbc.co.uk/dna/h2g2/A378209

http://www.digitaljournal.com/article/296201

http://www.pollsb.com/polls/p3268-ride_nudist_airline#stats

http://gocalifornia.about.com/cs/clothingoptional/a/nudebeachguide.htm

http://www.travelerstipsnpics.com/06/ten-best-nude-beaches-in-the-world/

http://vadimage.wordpress.com/2011/02/02/top-10-fkk-events-2011-from-news-at/

http://www.thaindian.com/newsportal/world-news/list-of-10-best-places-to-get-naked-in-2011-revealed_100501304.html

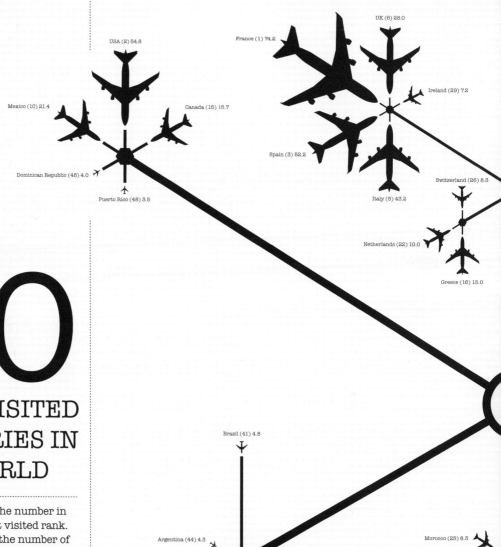

the

# 50

## MOST VISITED COUNTRIES IN THE WORLD

For each country, the number in brackets is its most visited rank. This is followed by the number of tourists (millions) that visited the country in 2009.

USA (2) 54.8

France (1) 74.2

UK (6) 28.0

Ireland (29) 7.2

Mexico (10) 21.4

Canada (15) 15.7

Spain (3) 52.2

Switzerland (26) 8.3

Dominican Republic (45) 4.0

Netherlands (22) 10.0

Puerto Rico (48) 3.5

Italy (5) 43.2

Greece (16) 15.0

Brazil (41) 4.8

Argentina (44) 4.3

Morocco (28) 8.3

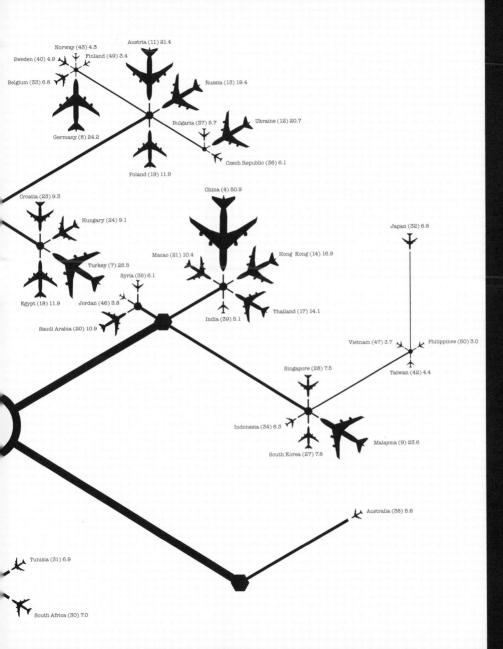

Norway (48) 4.3
Sweden (40) 4.9
Finland (49) 3.4
Austria (11) 21.4
Belgium (33) 6.8
Russia (13) 19.4
Germany (8) 24.2
Bulgaria (37) 5.7
Ukraine (12) 20.7
Czech Republic (36) 6.1
Poland (19) 11.9
Croatia (23) 9.3
Hungary (24) 9.1
China (4) 50.9
Japan (32) 6.8
Macao (21) 10.4
Hong Kong (14) 16.9
Turkey (7) 25.5
Syria (35) 6.1
Egypt (18) 11.9
Jordan (46) 3.8
Thailand (17) 14.1
India (39) 5.1
Saudi Arabia (20) 10.9
Vietnam (47) 3.7
Philippines (50) 3.0
Singapore (28) 7.5
Taiwan (42) 4.4
Indonesia (34) 6.3
Malaysia (9) 23.6
South Korea (27) 7.8
Australia (38) 5.6
Tunisia (31) 6.9
South Africa (30) 7.0

# International Tourist Arrivals
## (millions)

2009

- Europe.....................54.7%
- Asia and the Pacific.......20.1%
- Americas...................16.4%
- Middle East.................3.4%
- Africa......................3.0%
- Origin not specified.........2.4%

2008

- Europe.....................55.2%
- Asia and the Pacific.......19.7%
- Americas...................16.4%
- Middle East.................3.6%
- Africa......................3.0%
- Origin not specified.........2.4%

The World Tourism rankings are compiled by the World Tourism Organization (UNWTO).

# CRAWLING SNACKS *from around the world*

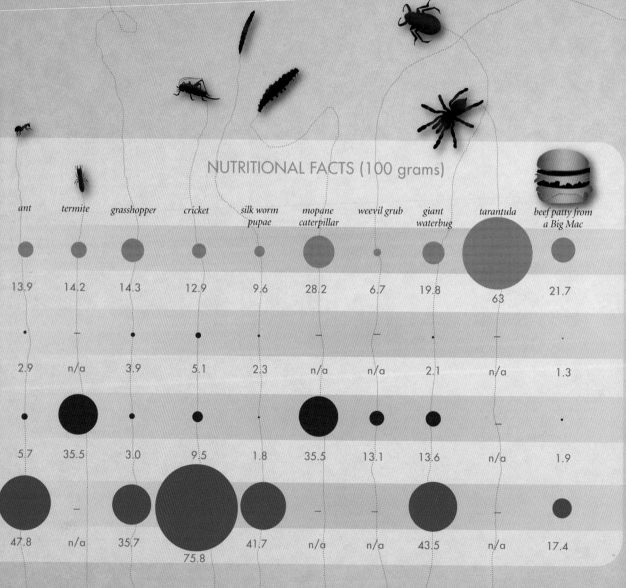

## NUTRITIONAL FACTS (100 grams)

| | ant | termite | grasshopper | cricket | silk worm pupae | mopane caterpillar | weevil grub | giant waterbug | tarantula | beef patty from a Big Mac |
|---|---|---|---|---|---|---|---|---|---|---|
| | 13.9 | 14.2 | 14.3 | 12.9 | 9.6 | 28.2 | 6.7 | 19.8 | 63 | 21.7 |
| | 2.9 | n/a | 3.9 | 5.1 | 2.3 | n/a | n/a | 2.1 | n/a | 1.3 |
| | 5.7 | 35.5 | 3.0 | 9.5 | 1.8 | 35.5 | 13.1 | 13.6 | n/a | 1.9 |
| | 47.8 | n/a | 35.7 | 75.8 | 41.7 | n/a | n/a | 43.5 | n/a | 17.4 |

# 1,681 insect species are eaten in:

**11** countries in Europe

**23** countries in the Americas

**36** countries in Africa

**29** countries in Asia

**14** countries in Oceania

PROTEIN (g)

CARBOHYDRATE (g)

IRON (mg)

CALCIUM (mg)

*Entomophagy* is the practice of eating insects.

Over **2,500,000,000** people around the world eat insects daily.

In North Thailand, the top reason for eating insects is: "*Insects are tasty.*"

The Food and Agricultural Organization (FAO) is promoting insects as a future food source as they are *highly nutritious* and much more *environmentally friendly* than cattle or chicken.

SOURCES:
Man Eating Bugs: The Art
and Science of Eating Insects,
by Peter Menzel and Faith D'Aluisio
http://www.planetscott.com/babes/nutrition.asp
http://www.hollowtop.com/finl_html/finl.html
http://www.ca.uky.edu/entomology/dept/bugfood2.asp
http://www.suite101.com/content/insects-as-alternative-food-a278697
http://www.riverdeep.net/current/2002/03/030402_eatingbugs.jhtml
http://www.essortment.com/entomophagy-using-insects-food-source-22027.html
http://caloriecount.about.com/calories-mcdonalds-big-mac-all-beef-i53841
http://www.fao.org/newsroom/en/news/2008/1000791/index.html
http://www.smallstockfoods.com/about/
http://www.food-insects.com/
http://www.thaibugs.com/?page_id=723
http://en.wikipedia.org/wiki/Entomophagy

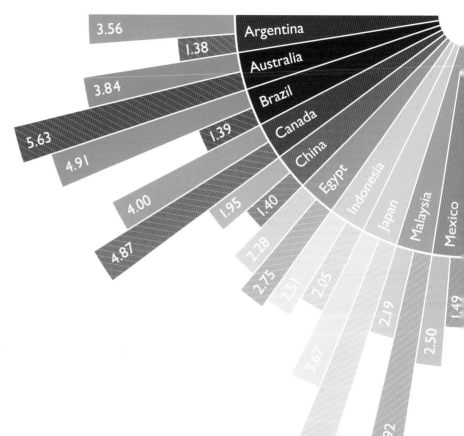

## Value of the Dollar in
## Burgers & Beers

As a traveller, it's an essential skill to be able to quickly work out how the value of a dollar varies from one country to another. Compare your destinations: this chart shows the relative prices, in US dollars, of a fast-food chain burger (lighter) and a local beer (darker, striped).

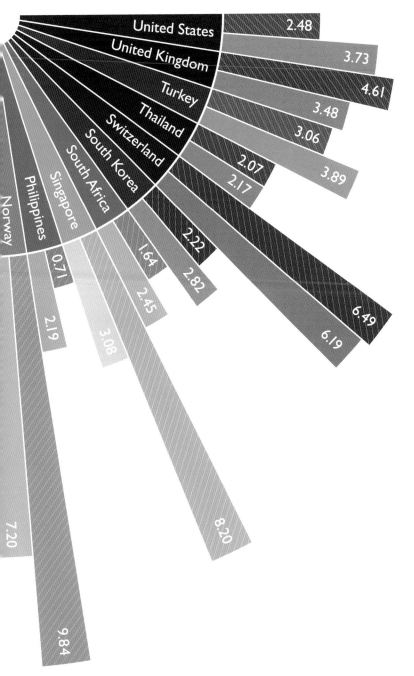

United States 2.48

United Kingdom 3.73

Turkey 4.61

Thailand 3.48

Switzerland 3.06

South Korea 2.07

South Africa 2.17

Singapore 2.22

Philippines 1.64

Norway 2.82

6.49

6.19

0.71

2.45

3.08

2.19

7.20

8.20

9.84

Sources:   bigmacindex.org
pintprice.com

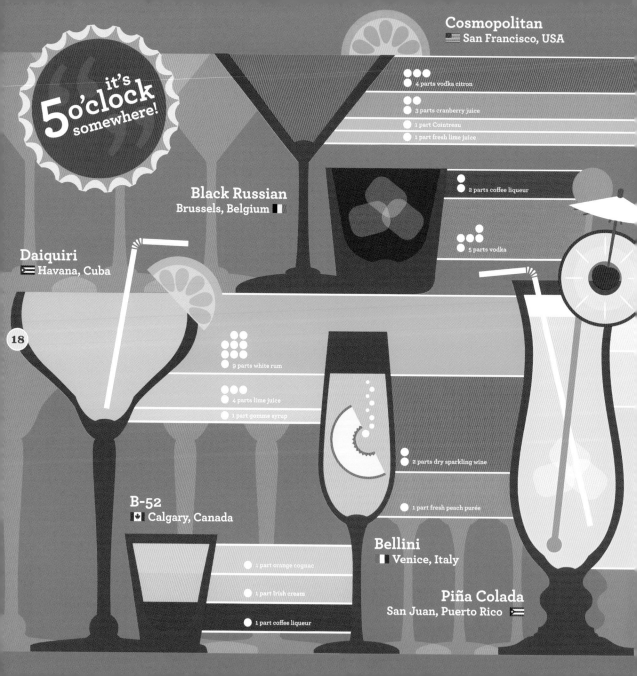

it's **5 o'clock** somewhere!

## Cosmopolitan
🇺🇸 San Francisco, USA

4 parts vodka citron

3 parts cranberry juice

1 part Cointreau

1 part fresh lime juice

## Black Russian
**Brussels, Belgium** 🇧🇪

2 parts coffee liqueur

5 parts vodka

## Daiquiri
🇨🇺 Havana, Cuba

18

9 parts white rum

4 parts lime juice

1 part gomme syrup

## B-52
🇨🇦 Calgary, Canada

1 part orange cognac

1 part Irish cream

1 part coffee liqueur

## Bellini
🇮🇹 Venice, Italy

2 parts dry sparkling wine

1 part fresh peach purée

## Piña Colada
San Juan, Puerto Rico 🇵🇷

## Bloody Mary
🇺🇸 New York, USA

6 parts tomato juice

3 parts vodka

1 part lemon juice

## Blue Lagoon
🇺🇸 Unknown, USA

1 part blue curaçao

1 part vodka

4 parts lemonade

## Kamikaze
🇯🇵 Unknown, Japan

1 part vodka

1 part triple sec

1 part lime juice

## Singapore Sling
Singapore, Singapore 🇸🇬

16 parts pineapple juice

8 parts gin

6 parts lemon juice

4 parts cherry liqueur

2 parts grenadine

1 part Cointreau, 1 part DOM Bénédictine, 1 part Angostura Bitters

## Whiskey Sour
Unknown, England 🏴󠁧󠁢󠁥󠁮󠁧󠁿

4.5 parts bourbon whiskey

3 parts lemon juice

1.5 parts gomme syrup

1 dash egg white

Source: International Bartenders Association (www.iba-world.com)

# Top Trails

Colorado Trail (USA)
Kungsleden (Sweden)
Haute Route (France and Switzerland)
Mount Kilimanjaro (Tanzania)
Inca Trail (Peru)

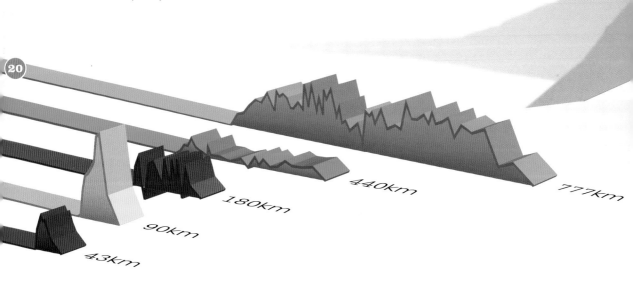

777km

440km

180km

90km

43km

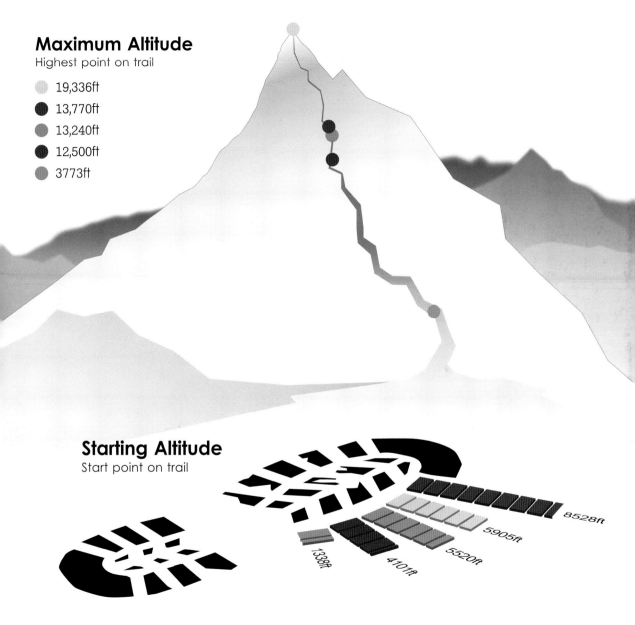

# Maximum Altitude
Highest point on trail

- 19,336ft
- 13,770ft
- 13,240ft
- 12,500ft
- 3773ft

## Starting Altitude
Start point on trail

1338ft

4101ft

5520ft

5905ft

8528ft

Sources: wikipedia.org, nationalgeographic.com, incatrailperu.com, coloradotrail.org, mtkilimanjarologue.com

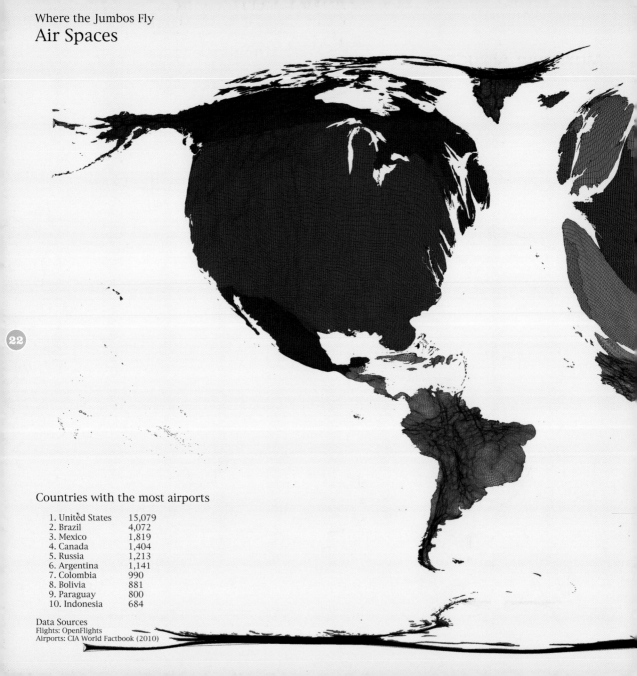

# Air Spaces

## Countries with the most airports

| | | |
|---|---|---|
| 1. | United States | 15,079 |
| 2. | Brazil | 4,072 |
| 3. | Mexico | 1,819 |
| 4. | Canada | 1,404 |
| 5. | Russia | 1,213 |
| 6. | Argentina | 1,141 |
| 7. | Colombia | 990 |
| 8. | Bolivia | 881 |
| 9. | Paraguay | 800 |
| 10. | Indonesia | 684 |

Data Sources
Flights: OpenFlights
Airports: CIA World Factbook (2010)

A map showing the most crowded skies in the world

Each grid cell on the map is related to the same amount of space in the physical world. The size of a grid cell reflects the density of airline routes in that area. The larger a grid cell, the more flights are estimated to go along there.

# IS THE GRASS GREENER ON THE OTHER SIDE?

They say there's no place like home but for millions worldwide, adopting a new home in a foreign land signifies a new lease of life. We examine the migration patterns of people all over the world.

**1** in every **33** persons in the world is a migrant.

Sources: International Organization for Migration (www.iom.int), United Kingdom Office for National Statistics (www.statistics.gov.uk), Department of Immigration and Citizenship Australia (www.immi.gov.au), Wikipedia (http://bit.ly/nL89fF).

# GOING WHERE THE WIND BLOWS

A breakdown of preferred migration destinations according to country.

SLOVAKIA
2.4%

TURKEY
1.9%

QATAR
# 87%

JAPAN
1.7%

JORDAN
# 46%

INDIA
0.4%

AT
0.1%,
INDONESIA
HAS THE LOWEST
PERCENTAGE OF
MIGRANTS.

SAUDI
ARABIA
## 28%

UAE
# 70%

NIGERIA
0.7%

SINGAPORE
## 41%

SOUTH
AFRICA
3.7%

## UK

AUSTRALIA
SPAIN
GERMANY
FRANCE
USA

## AUSTRALIA

UK
USA
NZ
SINGAPORE
UAE
HONG KONG

# 214 MILLION

international migrants worldwide today, compared to 150 million in the year 2000.

Together, migrants worldwide would form the world's fifth most populous country.

THAT IS EQUIVALENT TO THE POPULATION OF
BRAZIL

# CORNETTO & CAPPUCCINO?

## QUICK GUIDE TO TYPICAL ITALIAN
## BREAKFASTS: REGION BY REGION

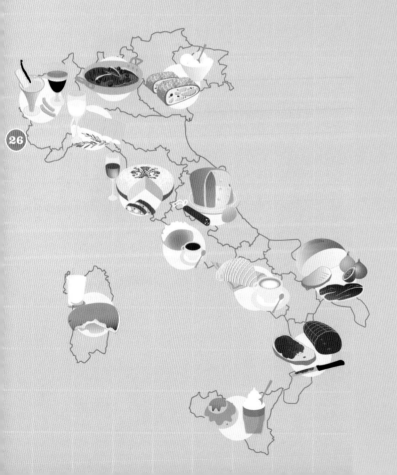

### Piemonte

*Zabaione* with red *krumiri* and *bicerin*, a traditional hot coffee native to Turin

### Toscana

*Schiacciata alla fiorentina* and *cantuccini* to dip in a glass of sweet *vin santo*

### Campania

*Sfogliatella napoletana*, (try both *riccia* and *frolla*) and *cappuccino*

## Lombardia

The *cassuela* is a typical winter meat
stew suitable at all times of the day

## Veneto

Apple and raisin strudel
with vanilla ice cream

## Liguria

*Focaccia alla genovese*, with a sip of
*Bianchetta Genovese*, typical local wine

## Umbria

Easter breakfast in Umbria: *torta di
formaggio* with *corallina*, and eggs

## Lazio

*Maritozzo* with whipped cream
(or chocolate) and *espresso lungo*

## Sardegna

*Seadas* (fried crepes with honey
and pecorino cheese) and goat's milk

## Puglia

Toasted bread, fresh figs
and cured ham

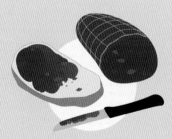

## Calabria

Bread and *'nduja*, a spicy spreadable
sausage made with pork

## Sicilia

Dip a *brioche* into a *granita di caffè con
panna*, a coffee sorbet with whipped cream

# DANGER

**Alaska, USA**
**Novarupta** was the site of the largest volcanic eruption of the 20th century.

**Hawaii, USA**
The world's largest (by volume) and most active volcanoes, **Mauna Loa** and **Kīlauea**, are found in Hawai'i Volcanoes National Park, which received over 1.3 million visitors in 2010.

Iconic **Mount Fuji** is extensively depicted in art and is widely recognized as a symbol of Japan. Climbing the volcano is viewed as a rite of passage for many Japanese.

**Mount Pinatubo** violently erupted in 1991, killing over 800 people and forever altering the landscape. A crater lake formed at the top has since become a tourist destination, where visitors can swim in its warm waters.

# Visiting
# Volcanoes
## In the Ring of Fire

Hundreds of volcanoes, including the majority of the active volcanoes in the world, are found in a circular region around the Pacific Ocean known as the Pacific Ring of Fire.

**Indonesia**
Seventy-six historically active volcanoes are found in Indonesia – the most of any country in the world. Several are destinations for hiking enthusiasts; **Mount Bromo**, for instance, is so popular that a staircase was built up the side of its volcanic crater.

**Vanuatu**
**Mount Yasur** is one of the world's most accessible volcanoes. Eruptions can be viewed from the rim of the volcanic crater.

**New Zealand**
The most active volcano in the country, **Mount Ruapehu**, is also the largest ski resort in New Zealand.

**Antarctica**
Commercial sightseeing flights between New Zealand and Antarctica once flew past **Mount Erebus** (off map), the southernmost active volcano in the world. But in 1979 the route was abruptly cancelled after Air New Zealand Flight 901 crashed into the base of the volcano, tragically killing all 257 on board.

**24,400m** – Height of ash cloud during 1980 eruption of **Mount St. Helens**

The top of **Mount St. Helens** was blown away in a catastrophic 1980 eruption. The mountain is now a designated national monument that educates visitors on the natural history of this volcano.

## Volume of erupted volcanic ash

The three largest eruptions of the 20th century are dwarfed by the eruptions of the supervolcano that created the present-day Yellowstone geothermal region in Wyoming, USA.

**Novarupta**, USA
12km$^3$ in 1912

**Mount Pinatubo**, Philippines
4.8km$^3$ in 1991

**Mount St. Helens**, USA
0.4km$^3$ in 1980

**Yellowstone
(Huckleberry Ridge)
USA**
2,450km$^3$
2.1 million years ago

Circles depict area of 1km-deep ash field of expelled material from each eruption.

### Colombia
The great heights that volcanoes can reach often create a mix of fire and ice, such as the glacier-capped summit of **Nevado del Ruiz**. In 1985 an eruption caused this ice to melt, generating lahars that destroyed the city of Armero, killing over 20,000 people.

Due to its height, **Nevados Ojos del Salado** has been used for record-setting ascents in an automobile.

**6,893m** – **Nevados Ojos del Salado**, the highest volcano on earth

## Danger to plane travel
Volcanic ash can be sucked into jet engines where it melts and can lead to engine failure. Consequently, flight cancellations are common when volcanoes erupt.

### Chile
In June 2011 the **Puyehue-Cordón Caulle** volcanic complex erupted, sending an ash cloud around the southern hemisphere that caused the cancellations of flights from Chile to New Zealand.

**2,550m** – **Mount St. Helens**

**361m** – **Mount Yasur**

Ground level

SOURCE: US Geological Survey, US National Park Service

# THE MANY HARDSHIPS OF LEWIS & CLARK
## AND THE CORPS OF DISCOVERY:
### THE NORTHWEST PASSAGE, THEN AND NOW

IN 1803, PRESIDENT OF THE UNITED STATES THOMAS JEFFERSON PURCHASED THE LOUISIANA TERRITORY FROM NAPOLEON BONAPARTE OF FRANCE FOR $15 MILLION (A COST OF ROUGHLY 3 CENTS PER ACRE). THIS ADDED 820,000 SQUARE MILES TO THE COUNTRY, EFFECTIVELY DOUBLING ITS SIZE. IN AN EFFORT TO SURVEY THE ACQUISITION AND DISCOVER THE FABLED "NORTH-WEST PASSAGE" – A WATERWAY WHICH WOULD LEAD TO THE PACIFIC OCEAN – JEFFERSON SENT MERIWETHER LEWIS AND WILLIAM CLARK ON A JOURNEY UP THE MISSOURI RIVER WITH 31 OTHER MEN DUBBED THE CORPS OF DISCOVERY. THESE ARE SOME OF THE MANY HARDSHIPS THEY ENDURED, AND HOW THEY COMPARE TO THE PRESENT.

GREAT FALLS

CLAIMED BY SPAIN, ENGLAND, RUSSIA, US

US AND ENGLAND

BISMARCK NORTH DAKOTA

PIERRE SOUTH DAKOTA

INDIANA TERRITORY

UNITED STATES OF 1804

CLAIMED BY SPAIN

KANSAS CITY

ST LOUIS

LOUISIANA PURCHASE

INDIANA TERRITORY

CLAIMED BY US AND SPAIN

SPANISH FLORIDA

## SUPPLIES

THE CORPS LEFT ST LOUIS HAVING SPENT $2,324 ON SUPPLIES, WHICH INCLUDED AN ESTIMATED 120-300 GALLONS OF WHISKEY. EACH MEMBER GOT 4 OUNCES PER DAY, BUT THE LAST OF IT WAS CONSUMED AT GREAT FALLS ON JULY 4, 1805. **TOO FAR FROM ANHEUSER-BUSCH CIVILIZATION** NOW CALLS ST LOUIS **TO DESERT** ITS HOME. IN 2006 IT PRODUCED OVER THAT'S 26 BARRELS FOR EVERY PERSON IN THE **157 MILLION** STATE OF MISSOURI **BARRELS OF BEER**

## 100 LASHES

FOR CRIMES SUCH AS BEING MUTINOUS, GOING AWOL OR STEALING WHISKEY, THE PUNISHMENT WAS A NUMBER OF LASHES ACROSS THE BARE BACK WITH WILLOW STICKS OR A RIFLE'S RAMROD. PRIVATE HALL RECEIVED 100 LASHES FOR STEALING WHISKEY NEAR PRESENT-DAY KANSAS CITY CURRENT PENALTIES FOR SHOPLIFTING IN MISSOURI

UP TO ONE YEAR IN JAIL AND A $1000 FINE

## RUSH'S THUNDERBOLTS

WERE A POWERFUL LAXATIVE USED AS A CURE-ALL AT THE TIME. MEMBERS OF THE CORPS USED THEM TO TREAT DYSENTERY. OUCH. TODAY, COMMON TREATMENTS FOR TRAVELERS DIARRHEA INCLUDE BISMUTHS (SUCH AS PEPTO-BISMOL OR KAOPECTATE), WHICH CAN BE FOUND AT MOST TRUCK STOPS FOR A FEW DOLLARS. THE MECHANISM BY WHICH THESE MEDICINES APPEAR TO WORK ON THE DIGESTIVE TRACT IS STILL LARGELY UNDOCUMENTED.

## MOSQUITOES

IMMENSELY NUMEROUS AND TROUBLESOME BY LEWIS' ACCOUNT, THEY KEPT THE DOG UP HOWLING ALL NIGHT AND AT TIMES WERE SO THICK THAT THE CORPS COULD BARELY OPEN THEIR MOUTHS TO EAT OR RAISE THEIR RIFLES TO SHOOT.

DEET IS A MODERN MOSQUITO REPELLENT THAT WAS DEVELOPED BY THE US ARMY DURING WORLD WAR II. BOTH MALE AND FEMALE MOSQUITOES INTENSELY DISLIKE THE **SMELL**

## TETON SIOUX

THE TETON SIOUX OCCUPIED TWO VILLAGES NEAR WHAT IS NOW PIERRE, SOUTH DAKOTA, AND WERE KNOWN BY BOTH TRADERS AND NEIGHBORING TRIBES FOR BEING QUITE

# AGGRESSIVE,

DEMANDING LARGE GIFTS FROM ALL MERCHANTS WHO TRIED TO PASS BY. THE CORPS NARROWLY AVOIDED ARMED CONFLICT WITH THIS TRIBE.

## SACAGAWEA

THIS YOUNG SHOSHONI WOMAN AND HER INFANT SON, JEAN BAPTISTE, ACCOMPANIED THE CORPS ON THE JOURNEY BEYOND THE MANDAN VILLAGES AS PART OF A CHAIN OF TRANSLATORS. SHE HAD TO CARRY THE CHILD ON HER BACK FOR THOUSANDS OF MILES. CURRENTLY, INFANTS TRAVEL IN CHILD SAFETY SEATS, WHICH **REDUCE RISK OF DEATH BY 71%.** BOOSTER SEATS ARE RECOMMENDED FOR CHILDREN UNTIL THEY ARE **8 YEARS OLD OR 4'9" TALL.**

# BILIOUS CHOLIC

WAS THE DIAGNOSIS OF THE ILL SERGEANT CHARLES FLOYD BY THE CORPS. HE DIED ON AUGUST 20, 1804, THE ONLY MEMBER OF THE CORPS TO DIE DURING THE TWO-YEAR JOURNEY.

# 6 MONTHS

IS THE LENGTH OF TIME IT TOOK FOR THE CORPS TO REACH THE MANDAN VILLAGES NEAR PRESENT-DAY BISMARCK, NORTH DAKOTA, FROM THE MOUTH OF THE MISSOURI RIVER. THEY TRAVELED 1600 MILES IN A 55'-LONG KEELBOAT BY SAILING, ROWING, USING POLES, AND PULLING THE BOAT UPRIVER WITH ROPES. CURRENT TRAVEL TIMES FROM

→ **ST LOUIS TO BISMARCK**
✈ **4 HOURS, 10 MINUTES** ←
🚗 **16 HOURS, 9 MINUTES** ←
🚲 **85 HOURS** ←

AVERAGE TIME

MANY SIOUX NOW LIVE ON THE 3,469 SQUARE-MILE PINE RIDGE RESERVATION. IT IS LARGER THAN DELAWARE AND RHODE ISLAND COMBINED. THE PREDOMINANT FORM OF TRAVEL IS **WALKING** OR

## HITCHHIKING

## HAIL

ON JUNE 29, 1805, LEWIS WROTE, "THE MEN... WERE SORELY MAWLED WITH THE HAIL WHICH WAS SO LARGE AND DRIVEN WITH SUCH FORCE BY THE WIND THAT IT NOCKED MANY OF THEM DOWN... MOST OF THEM WERE BLEEDING FREELY AND COMPLAINED OF BEING MUCH BRUISED." TODAY, HAIL STORMS CAUSE MORE THAN **$1.6 BILLION** IN DAMAGE IN THE US EACH YEAR.

MEDICAL HISTORIANS HAVE DETERMINED THAT FLOYD'S DEATH WAS THE RESULT OF A **RUPTURED APPENDIX** ODDS A PERSON WILL DIE FROM APPENDICITIS IN A YEAR (US–2004)
**1 IN 648,200**

# SPANISH INTERCEPT

THE SPANISH, AFRAID THAT THE UNITED STATES HAD DESIGNS ON MEXICO, TRIED SEVERAL TIMES TO INTERCEPT THE CORPS OF DISCOVERY. **THEY WERE UNSUCCESSFUL.** TODAY, POLICE INTERCEPT MILLIONS OF SPEEDERS IN THE US EACH YEAR.

AVERAGE FINES PER US OFFICER PER YEAR **$300,000**
AVERAGE SALARY PER US OFFICER PER YEAR **$75,000**

SPEEDING ECONOMICS

APPROXIMATE RETURN ON INVESTMENT $225,000
$10,000

# GRIZZLY BEARS

IN NORTH DAKOTA, THE HIDATSA PEOPLE DESCRIBED THE HUGE GRIZZLIES THE CORPS WOULD FIND IN WHAT IS NOW MONTANA. AFTER BEING **CHASED ACROSS THE PLAINS** BY SEVERAL OF THE GRIZZLIES, LEWIS WROTE THAT THE CORPS' CURIOSITY HAD BEEN "PRETTY MUCH SATISFIED."

CURRENT GRIZZLY **POPULATION** CONTINENTAL US

**ABOUT 1000**

## BITTERROOT MOUNTAINS

THE CORPS RAN OUT OF FOOD AND HAD TO EAT HORSES TO SURVIVE. THEY WERE SO HUNGRY THAT THEY ATE ANYTHING THEY COULD GET THEIR HANDS ON. THEY EVEN **ATE CANDLES**

TODAY, US ROUTE 12 PASSES THROUGH THIS AREA, ALONG WHICH THERE ARE MANY PLACES FOR A TRAVELER TO DINE. AS OF 2006, THERE WERE MORE THAN 300,000 FAST FOOD RESTAURANTS IN THE US.

US SPENDING ON **FAST FOOD**
1970 $6B
2006 $142B

US dollars are used throughout. Sources: wikipedia.org, pbs.org/lewisandclark/, nationalgeographic.com/lewisandclark/, lewisclark.net, lewis-clark.org, lewis-clark-trail.us, linkcenterfoundation.org, http://www.bookofodds.com/Health-Illness/Gastrointestinal/Articles/A0182-Appendicitis, facts.randomhistory.com/2009/06/27_fast-food.html

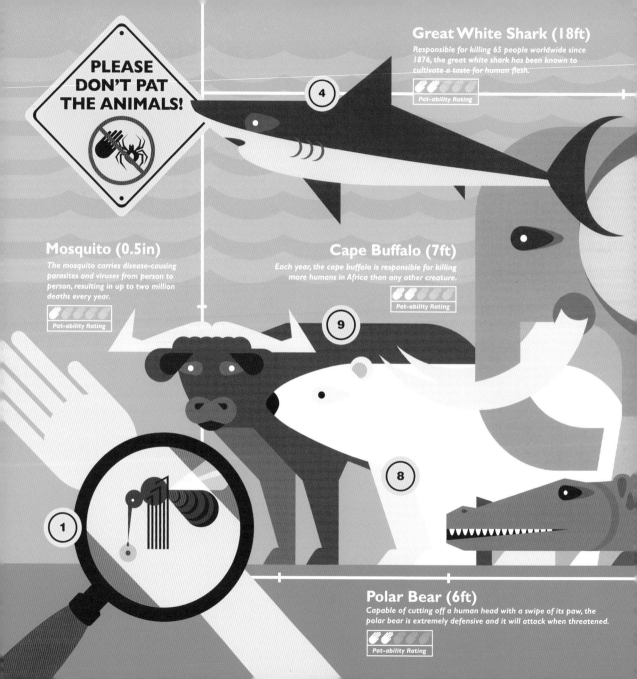

**PLEASE DON'T PAT THE ANIMALS!**

# Great White Shark (18ft)

Responsible for killing 65 people worldwide since 1876, the great white shark has been known to cultivate a taste for human flesh.

*Pat-ability Rating*

# Mosquito (0.5in)

The mosquito carries disease-causing parasites and viruses from person to person, resulting in up to two million deaths every year.

*Pat-ability Rating*

# Cape Buffalo (7ft)

Each year, the cape buffalo is responsible for killing more humans in Africa than any other creature.

*Pat-ability Rating*

# Polar Bear (6ft)

Capable of cutting off a human head with a swipe of its paw, the polar bear is extremely defensive and it will attack when threatened.

*Pat-ability Rating*

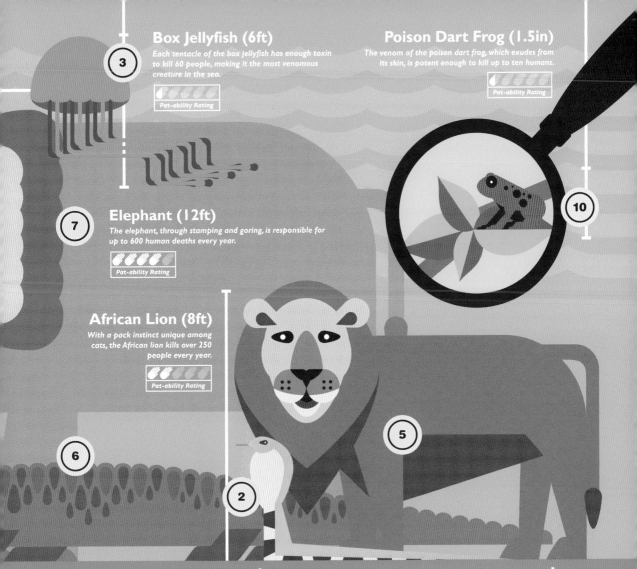

### Box Jellyfish (6ft)

Each tentacle of the box jellyfish has enough toxin to kill 60 people, making it the most venomous creature in the sea.

**3**

Pat-ability Rating

### Poison Dart Frog (1.5in)

The venom of the poison dart frog, which exudes from its skin, is potent enough to kill up to ten humans.

**10**

Pat-ability Rating

### Elephant (12ft)

The elephant, through stamping and goring, is responsible for up to 600 human deaths every year.

**7**

Pat-ability Rating

### African Lion (8ft)

With a pack instinct unique among cats, the African lion kills over 250 people every year.

Pat-ability Rating

**6**

**2**

**5**

### Saltwater Crocodile (23ft)

An opportunistic hunter, the saltwater crocodile is responsible for over 2,000 deaths every year.

Pat-ability Rating

### Asian Cobra (6ft)

Bites from the Asian cobra cause a majority of the 50,000 snakebite deaths that occur each year in India.

Pat-ability Rating

Telegraph, Top 10 Deadliest Animals On The Planet (www.telegraph.co.uk)

# Vaccination Recommendations

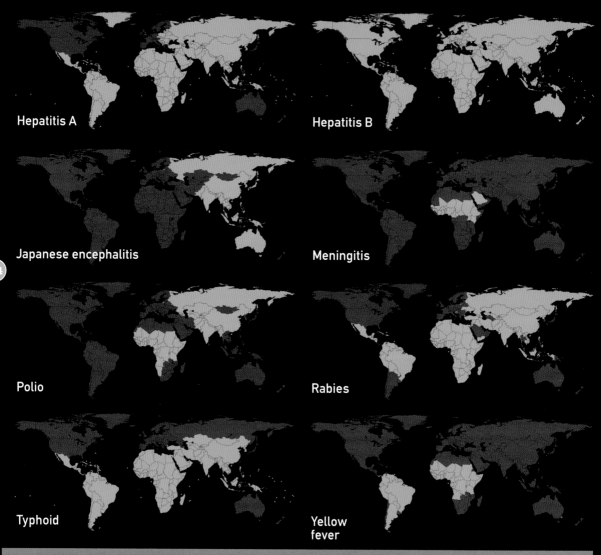

Hepatitis A

Hepatitis B

Japanese encephalitis

Meningitis

Polio

Rabies

Typhoid

Yellow fever

34

Blue countries show where the specified vaccination is recommended. Countries in grey have little to no risk of the disease. Vaccination and TD information from the United States Centers for Disease Control and the World Health Organization.

# Travelers' Diarrhea

Travelers' diarrhea is the most common illness to affect travelers. Often, infection is the result of ingesting fecally contaminated food or water.

## *Affects*

at least
## 20%
of all travelers

## *People* AT HIGHER RISK

· Young adults
· Immunosuppressed people
· People with IBS
· People with diabetes
· People taking H-2 blockers or antacids

## *Places* AT HIGHER RISK

· Africa
· Asia
· Latin America
· Middle East

## *Food & Drink* AT HIGHER RISK

Tap water

Ice

Unpasteurized milk

Dairy products

## *Preventative* MEASURES

Avoid eating foods or drinking beverages purchased from street vendors or other establishments where unhygienic conditions are present.

Avoid eating raw or undercooked meat and seafood.

Avoid eating raw fruits and vegetables unless you peel them.

Sources: www.who.int/ith/chapters/en/index.html, apps.who.int/ghodata/, wwwnc.cdc.gov/travel/destinations/list.htm, and www.cdc.gov/ncidod/dbmd/diseaseinfo/travelersdiarrhea_g.htm

# WHO DO YOU CALL?

Wherever you are, whatever trouble you're in, there's bound to be an emergency phone number you can dial for help.

This infographic shows the spectrum of emergency numbers across the world – keep it handy, just in case!

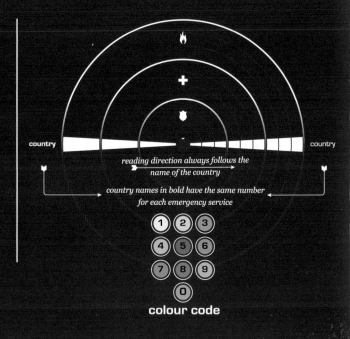

country

country

*reading direction always follows the name of the country*

*country names in bold have the same number for each emergency service*

colour code

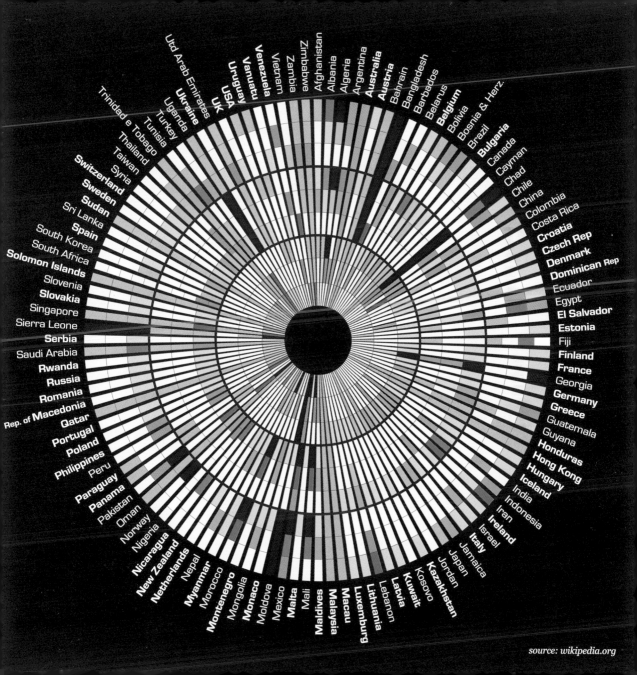

source: wikipedia.org

# hello India!

In a country where more than 2000 dialects are spoken, getting around can become complicated. Interact with locals by learning how to say HELLO in the official language of each state in India. Also learn about the origin of each language and how they compare to Hindi (422 million speakers) and English (220 million speakers), the two most widely spoken languages in the country.

**JAMMU & KASHMIR |** Urdu

HINDI
ENGLISH
52 MILLION

اسلام و علیکم | as-salam-wa-alaikum

**PUNJAB |** Punjabi

HINDI
ENGLISH
29 MILLION

ਸਤਿ ਸ੍ਰੀ ਅਕਾਲ। | sat-sri-akal

**GUJARAT |** Gujarati

HINDI
ENGLISH
46 MILLION

નમસ્કાર | na-mas-kar

ALSO OFFICIAL: HINDI

**MAHARASHTRA |** Marathi

HINDI
ENGLISH
72 MILLION

नमस्कार | na-mas-kar

ALSO OFFICIAL: ENGLISH

**GOA |** Konkani

HINDI
ENGLISH
7.6 MILLION

नमस्कार | na-mas-kar

**KARNATAKA |** Kannada

HINDI
ENGLISH
38 MILLION

ನಮಸ್ಕಾರ | na-mas-kara

**KERALA |** Malayalam

HINDI
ENGLISH
33 MILLION

നമസ്കാരം | na-mas-kaa-rum

ALSO OFFICIAL: ENGLISH

**RAJASTHAN, UTTARAKHAND, MADHYA PRADESH, JHARKHAND, BIHAR, UTTAR PRADESH, HARYANA, HIMACHAL PRADESH** | Hindi

नमस्ते | na-mas-the

422 MILLION
HINDI
ENGLISH

ALSO SPOKEN IN THESE STATES: RAJASTHANI, URDU, SANSKRIT, SANTALI, MAITHILI, PUNJABI

**SIKKIM** | Nepali

नमस्कार | na-mas-kar

HINDI
ENGLISH
0.85 MILLION

**ASSAM, ARUNACHAL PRADESH** | Assamese

নমস্কাৰ | na-mas-kaara

HINDI
ENGLISH
13 MILLION

**NAGALAND, MEGHALAYA** | English

ENGLISH HINDI
220 MILLION

**MANIPUR** | Manipuri

Khurumjari | khoo-room-jari

HINDI
ENGLISH
1.5 MILLION

**TRIPURA** | Tripuri

Khulumo | khoo-loo-mo

HINDI
ENGLISH
0.85 MILLION

**MIZORAM** | Mizo

Chi-bai Bûk | chee-baai-book

HINDI
ENGLISH
1 MILLION

**WEST BENGAL** | Bengali

নমস্কার | no-maa-sh-kar

HINDI
ENGLISH
83 MILLION

ALSO OFFICIAL: ENGLISH, NEPALI

**CHHATTISGARH** | Chhattisgarhi

नमस्कार | na-mas-kar

HINDI
ENGLISH
11 MILLION

**ORISSA** | Oriya

ନମସ୍କର | na-mas-kara

HINDI
ENGLISH
33 MILLION

**ANDHRA PRADESH** | Telugu

నమస్కారమండి | na-mas-kara-mundi

HINDI
ENGLISH
74 MILLION

ALSO OFFICIAL: URDU

**TAMIL NADU** | Tamil

வணக்கம் | va-na-kum

HINDI
ENGLISH
61 MILLION

**ABC** | State name
Abc | Official language
abc | Pronunciation of 'hello'
| No. of speakers (as per 2001 census data)

| Indo-Aryan origin
| Dravidian origin
| Tibeto-Burman origin
— | State borders

NOTE | *The languages listed here are only the "official" languages for each state. There are many dialects and sub-dialects that are spoken in each of these regions.*

# Proud!
## *are you of your*
# nationality?

## 76,912 people in 54 countries answered...

**29.6%** Most prideful: Jordan

**0.1%**

**0.0%**

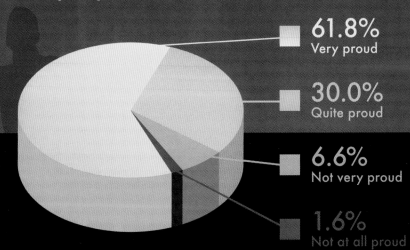

Worldwide average

**61.8%**
Very proud

**30.0%**
Quite proud

**6.6%**
Not very proud

**1.6%**
Not at all proud

**3.8%**

| North America | South America | Oceania | Asia | Greater Middle East | Africa | Europe |
|---|---|---|---|---|---|---|

d Values Survey 2005 2008. World Values Survey Association (www.worldvaluessurvey.org)

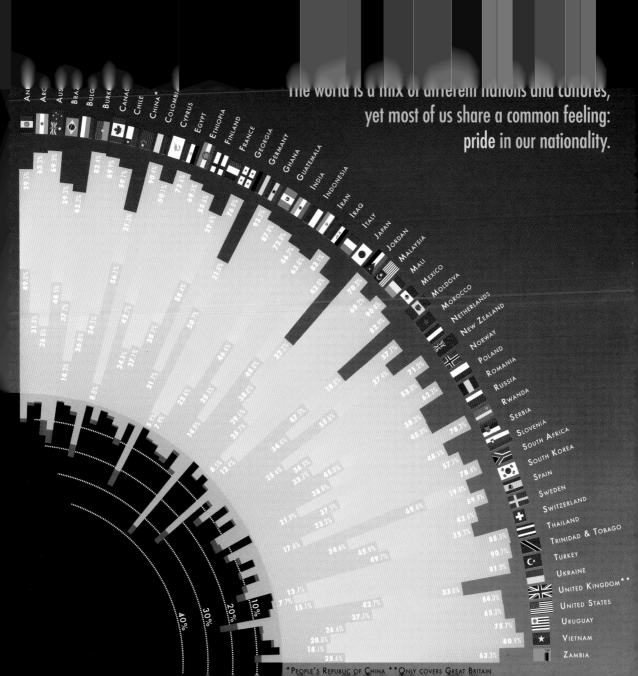

# TRAVEL LUGGAGE WOES

Millions of passengers' luggage items are mishandled globally every year. Take a look at the facts behind the drama passengers go through whenever they check-in a bag at the airport, and what you can do to prevent the same thing from happening to you.

## What Passengers Want

# 54.4%

say having checked-in baggage arrive promptly and safely contributes to an enjoyable journey.

# 4TH

most important factor associated with a pleasant trip – after on-time departures and arrivals, friendly ground staff and short queues.

## How Luggage Gets Lost

TRANSFER BAGGAGE MISHANDLING 52%

Transfer Baggage Mishandling - **52%**
Failure To Load - **16%**
Bag Switch/Security/Ticketing Error - **13%**
Airline/Customs/Weather Restrictions - **6%**
Loading/Offloading - **7%**
Arrival Station Mishandling - **3%**
Tagging Errors - **3%**

## Mishandled Luggage

# 25,025,000

mishandled bags globally in 2009.

# 1%

chance of your luggage getting lost or mishandled each time you hop on a plane.

### Comparing mishandled luggage yearly:

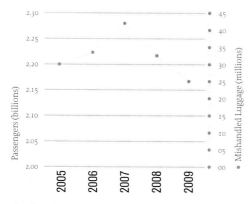

The drop has been attributed to a few factors – fewer people travelling, fewer checking in bags to avoid fees, and improvements in baggage handling systems.

# 23.8%

improvement from 2008.

## Cost Of Mishandling On Airlines

# 9.4BILLION

US dollars estimated in total airline losses in 2009, after losses of US$16.8 billion in 2008.

## Will I Ever See My Luggage Again?

# 98%

of lost and mishandled luggage will be reunited with its owner within 5 days.

## Top Tips For Airline Passengers

- Travel with only **carry-on luggage** if you can
- Put your **contact information** in and outside every bag
- **Customize** your bag to make it easy to identify
- **Keep valuable items with you**
- Make sure that the airline tag on your checked luggage is for the **correct destination**
- Ensure you **keep the stub** from your checked luggage
- **Head straight to the carousel** to prevent bag theft
- **Immediately report** the loss of checked luggage
- **Prepare to deal with a lost bag**

Sources

## TAKING CARE OF THE WORLD

There exists significant inequalities between developed and developing countries in our world. But many countries (with the means to do so) are working to restore the balance by offering financial assistance to those less fortunate. So just how much is being shared with friends in need, and in what areas are those donated resources being spent?

We've noted here some of the biggest donors, and the recipients of their assistance. The relative size of each donor-country's name is proportionate with their aid-spend as a percentage of their GDP.

Norway

Spain France Switzer

Italy

Netherlan

44

AFGHANISTAN
ALBANIA
ANGOLA
BANGLADESH
BENIN
BOLIVIA
BOSNIA & HERZEGOVINA
BOTSWANA
BRAZIL
BURKINA FASO
BURUNDI
CAMBODIA
CAMEROON
CAPE VERDE
CHAD
CHINA
COLOMBIA
CONGO (REP)
CONGO (DEM. REP)
COTE D'IVOIRE
EGYPT
EL SALVADOR
ETHIOPIA
GHANA
GUATEMALA
GUINEA-BISSAU
HAITI
HONDURAS
INDIA
INDONESIA
IRAQ
KENYA
KOSOVO
LAOS
LEBANON
LESOTHO
LIBERIA
MALAWI
MALAYSIA

**127.5** BILLION USD CONTRIBUTED ALTOGETHER BY DONORS IN 2009

**25** BILLION USD DONATED BY THE UNITED STATES, THE TOP DONOR IN 2009

**6** BILLION USD RECEIVED BY AFGHANISTAN, THE TOP RECIPIENT IN 2009

**SOURCE** WWW.OECD.ORG/DOCUMENT/11/0,3746,EN_2649_34447_2002187_1_1_1_1,00.HTML.
PLEASE REFER TO WEBSITE FOR FULL LIST OF DONORS AND RECIPIENTS

Sweden
Denmark
Canada
Portugal
United Kingdom
Australia
Germany
Japan
United States
Ireland
Korea
New Zealand
Greece
Austria

MALI · MAYOTTE · MONGOLIA · MOROCCO · MOZAMBIQUE · NAMIBIA · NEPAL · NICARAGUA · NIGER · NIGERIA · NIUE · **PAKISTAN** · **PALESTINE (ADM. AREAS)** · PAPUA NEW GUINEA · PERU · PHILIPPINES · RWANDA · SAO TOME & PRINCIPE · SENEGAL · SERBIA · SOLOMON IS. · SAMOA · SOMALIA · SOUTH AFRICA · SRI LANKA · SUDAN · SURINAME · SYRIA · **TANZANIA** · TIMOR LESTE · TOGO · TOKELAU · TONGA · TUNISIA · TURKEY · UGANDA · VANUATU · **VIETNAM** · ZAMBIA

TOP 10 RECIPIENTS
FOR 2009 IN **BOLD**

## EXPENDITURE BY SECTOR (%)

12 MULTISECTOR   1 DEBT   2 OTHER

50 SOCIAL    17 ECONOMIC    8 PRODUCTION    5 GENERAL PROGRAMME AID    5 HUMANITARIAN

# How to
# blend in

Wondering where in the world you will best blend in with the locals when ordering a coffee?

Want to know which languages to learn "one caffe latte please" in?

**Cappuccino** means "monk" in Italian, because this type of coffee was invented by...guess who?
Yep, an Italian monk.

**So, who consumes the most coffee per capita?**
Italians? Greeks? Turks?
Nope. Have a look (opposite) at the biggest coffee drinkers and where you should definitely order a coffee if you want to blend in...

Fine print: diagram is based on data from http://earthtrends.wri.org. Average consumption in kilograms per capita by country over the period 1998–2008. Countries that don't appear in the diagram either had insignificant results or no results available. Countries represented in larger font drink relatively more coffee per capita than those shown in smaller font. Finland drank the most (11.5 kilograms per capita – annual average) over the data period. •

Brazil is the biggest coffee producer in the world, and they also consume nearly 14 coffees every second.

Over a million coffees are made in Greece every day.

In Portugal 719 coffees are consumed every minute.

Americans drink over 700 coffees every minute.

In Iceland over 1500 coffees are made every minute.

The Britons drink 428 coffees every minute.

16 coffees are made every second in Italy.

In Finland almost 33 coffees are consumed every second!

belgium netherlands switzerland germany austria italy slovenia aruba france lebanon estonia iceland norway finland denmark canada brazil croatia sweden spain latvia czech republic armenia ireland united kingdom israel dominican republic hungary united states of america macedonia lithuania bulgaria australia puerto rico madagascar el salvador republic of korea kuwait venezuela qatar jordan cuba chile argentina saudi arabia suriname albania georgia philippines sudan tonga vanuatu vietnam côte d'ivoire swaziland uruguay madagascar paraguay peru mauritius mongolia indonesia turkey st lucia jamaica st vincent & grenadines grenada central african republic st kitts & nevis trinidad & tobago morocco mexico thailand uganda seychelles south africa solomon islands ecuador cayman islands jordan oman guatemala netherlands antilles haiti malta honduras panama ethiopia cape verde lao people's democratic republic syria tunisia russia nicaragua romania colombia bahamas slovakia new zealand poland algeria japan brunei darussalam greece cyprus portugal costa rica

A LOOK AT SOME
OF THE WORLD'S
MOST VISITED
DESTINATIONS...

PASSPORT

CHRIST THE REDEEMER
**0.6** MILLION
VISITORS PER YEAR

RIO DE JANEIRO

CAIRO

EIFFEL TOWER
**6.8** MILLION
VISITORS PER YEAR

PARIS

## STATUE OF LIBERTY
# 4.2 MILLION
#### VISITORS PER YEAR

## PYRAMIDS OF GIZA
# 3.0 MILLION
#### VISITORS PER YEAR

# NEW YORK

## THE LONDON EYE
# 3.5 MILLION
#### VISITORS PER YEAR

# LONDON

EARL GREY

# SYDNEY

## SYDNEY OPERA HOUSE
# 0.3 MILLION
#### VISITORS PER YEAR

Source: Forbes Traveler, 50 Most Visited Tourist Attractions (www.forbes.com/travel)

# SCENES OF DARKNESS

Travellers often find themselves drawn to places that have been witness to human suffering — this has become known as 'Dark Tourism'.

Dark Tourism is travel associated with destruction, tragedy, disaster and death. It's unclear why this kind of tourism has become so popular in recent times. Does it exist to satisfy curiosity? Does it promote remembrance and honouring of the dead? Does it serve to educate travellers, in the hope that such atrocities never happen again? Perhaps it just comes down to morbid fascination; but also, perhaps, travellers want to see how these places have rebuilt themselves.

This infographic looks at some key events from WWII to the present, and the reasons why their locations have become points of interest.

**2001** World Trade Center
New York, USA
3000+ casualties
3.6 million visitors

A series of coordinated suicide attacks by al-Qaeda, where two planes flew into the World Trade Centre (WTC) buildings and another into the Pentagon. Ground Zero (where the WTC once stood) remains a destination for those wishing to pay respects and understand more about the event. A 9/11 memorial was opened at Ground Zero on the 10th anniversary of the event.

**1992–1996** Bosnian War
Bosnia and Herzegovina
104,732 casualties
322,000 visitors annually

A territorial conflict as a result of the breakup of Yugoslavia, the Bosnian War was characterised by bitter fighting, indiscriminate shelling of cities and towns, ethnic cleansing, mass rape and genocide. The Siege of Sarajevo and the Srebrenica massacre typified the conflict.

**1997** Pont de l'Alma Tunnel Entrance
Paris, France
3 casualties

Initially named to commemorate the Battle of Alma during the Crimean War, it is now more famously known as the site where one of the icons of the 20th century, Princess Diana, died. The Flame of Liberty at one end of the bridge has become an unofficial memorial to her.

## Key

50

/// Countries with current conflict/s zones

1. Mexico
2. Colombia
3. Morocco
4. Mauritania
5. Senegal
6. Algeria
7. Mali
8. Libya
9. Chad
10. Nigeria
11. Central African Rep.
12. Sudan
13. Dem. Rep. Congo
14. Uganda
15. Somalia
16. Yemen
17. Iraq
18. Turkey
19. Israel/Palestine
20. Afghanistan
21. Pakistan
22. India
23. Burma
24. Thailand
25. Cambodia
26. Philippines
27. Korea

### Some Current Major Conflicts (1000+ deaths over 2010)

| Start of conflict | War/conflict | Location | Cumulative fatalities |
|---|---|---|---|
| 1967 | Naxalite-Maoist insurgency | India | 10,500+ |
| 1978 | Afghan civil war | Afghanistan | 600,000–2 million |
| 1991 | Somali civil war | Somalia | 300,000–400,000 |
| 2003 | War in Iraq | Iraq | 100,746–110,043 |
| 2004 | War in Northwest Pakistan | Pakistan | 30,452 |
| 2004 | Shi'ite insurgency in Yemen | Yemen | 12,833–16,439 |
| 2006 | Mexican drug war | Mexico | 36,226+ |
| 2009 | Sudanese nomadic conflicts | Sudan | 2000–2500 |
| 2011 | Libyan civil war | Libya | 10,000+ |

**1991–2002** Sierra Leone Civil War
Sierra Leone
Over 50,000 casualties
60,000 visitors annually

A civil war erupted between the government and the Revolutionary United Front because of increasing bitterness over years of rule by corrupt rulers and resentment of the rich who were controlling the wealth of the diamond mines. The rebels recruited children to fight, and many villagers suffered the fate of losing their limbs, which acted as a warning to others not to support the government or its forces. It lasted 11 years and displaced up to 4.5 million civilians. The fighting ended after a Nigeria-led force intervened.

**Sources** en.wikipedia.org, theage.com.au, tradingeconomics.com, icty.org, allafrica.com, cnntraveller.com, vhfcn.org/stat.htm, rjsmith.com/kia_tbl.html, thejakartaglobe.com/lifeandtimes, tourismcambodia.com, vacationideas.me/travel-tips/top-10-dark-tourism-destinations/, news.bbc.co.uk/2/hi, nationsonline.org,

**1945** Auschwitz–Birkenau Concentration Camp

Oswiecim, Poland

3 million casualties (2.5 million gassed, 500,000 from disease and starvation)

700,000 visitors annually

The largest and most infamous Nazi concentration and extermination camp, where trains of outcasts from all over Europe were delivered to their deaths. Birkenau was built when the capacity of Auschwitz was reached. Now a museum, it is a UNESCO World Heritage site.

**1986** Chernobyl Nuclear Disaster

Chernobyl, Ukraine

64 workers died; additional deaths up to 985,000

Located 128km northwest of Kiev, the world's worst nuclear disaster occurred when the emergency shutdown system at the Chernobyl nuclear power plant caused a sudden power output surge after routine testing, resulting in a number of explosions. Up to 350,500 people were evacuated and resettled. Official, government-approved day tours into affected areas began in 2011.

**1942** Death Railway

Kanchanaburi, Thailand to Moulmein, Burma

13,000 casualties

During WWII, Japanese troops set out to build a railway line to connect some of the outer regions of the country and create a route to further their march into Asia. The 416km-long railway took 16 months to complete and workers included foreign POWs. Alongside Asian slave labourers, the POWs suffered malnutrition, starvation and overworking, as well as having little or no medical and sanitary facilities. The most famous section of the railway is the bridge that spans the River Kwai.

**1990s to Present** North Korean Famine

North Korea

900,000 to 2.2 million deaths from starvation or hunger-related illnesses.

1500 Western and thousands of Asian visitors annually

Following the dissolution of the Soviet Union in the early 90s, North Korea went into industrial decline. It failed to recover from this and as a result it struggled to sustain its agricultural system. Major floods also contributed to the decline of its arable land. In 2011, North Koreans' daily food intake is approximately 700 calories/day as compared to a healthy European citizens' 2000–2500 calories/day.

**1945** 'Little Boy' and 'Fat Man' Atomic Bombs

Hiroshima and Nagasaki, Japan

245,000 casualties

1.17 million visitors to memorial centres annually

After months of intensive bombings of Japanese cities in WWII, two atomic bombs were deployed by the US. This resulted in Japan surrendering to the Allied Powers, ending the Pacific War. These remain the only times in which an atomic bomb was used in war.

**1989** Tiananmen Square Massacre

Beijing, China

1000 to 4000 casualties

Demonstrators, predominantly made up of students, staged a seven-week nonviolent protest at the square for continued economic reform and liberalisation. The People's Liberation Army took to the streets, firing indiscriminately to quell protestors.

**1955–1975** War in Vietnam

Vietnam

5.4 million casualties (military and civilian)

4.5 million visitors annually

Fought in two phases: first, between the Vietnamese and the French; second, between the South and North Vietnamese. The US involvement during the second phase was to prevent a communist takeover of South Vietnam, thereby preventing the realisation of their 'domino theory' in Southeast Asia. The Demilitarized Zone, Cu Chi tunnels and Dien Bien Phu are popular sites for visitors.

**1994** Rwandan Genocide

Kigali, Rwanda

800,000 casualties

1 million visitors annually

In the space of 100 days, one of the most horrific and widespread incidents of genocide took place. Sparked by the death of the Rwandan president, fighting broke out between the two country's two main ethnic groups (Hutus and Tutsis). Most of those killed were Tutsis and most of those who committed the violence were Hutus. A memorial was opened at the burial site of over 250,000 people in 2004, the 10th anniversary of the genocide.

**Present** Dharavi Slum

Mumbai, India

Casualties unknown

Home to almost 1 million people, Dharavi is the largest slum in Asia. Residents live amongst piling garbage and human waste with endless displays of poverty, disease and depressing living conditions. Tour operators donate part of their income into the community, but ironically it may be in their best interest for the slums to remain in their present state in order to generate revenue.

**1979** Cambodian Genocide

Cambodia

2 million casualties

2 million visitors annually

Led by the infamous Pol Pot, the Khmer Rouge regime lasted for 4 years, during which 25% of the population was killed. Political executions, torture, starvation and forced labour were features of the reign. Tuol Sleng Prison and the Killing Fields are poignant reminders of this dark period.

# Backpacking
## what to take?

**Duct tape**

May be used for repairing tears, covering blisters etc

**Multi-tool**

**Maintenance**

**Insect repellent**

**Towel**

**Soap**

**Toilet tissue**

**Dental care**

**Comfort**

**Tent**

**Sleeping bag & mat**

**Staying overnight?**

PACK

WEIGHT

**Flashlight**

**Whistle**

**Safety**

**First aid kit**

**Compass**

**Unfamiliar trail?**

**Map**

**GPS**

**Locator beacon**

## Equipment

**Type of terrain?**

**Uneven**

**Icy**

**Hiking poles**

**Crampons**

## Shelter

**Staying dry & warm is most critical**

(!) Death may occur within 2 hours of onset of hypothermia

**Weather forecast?**

**Cold**

**Rain**

**Sunshine**

**Insulated clothing**

**Rain cover**

**Plastic bags**

**Sunscreen**

**Clothing**

(!) Fair skin burns in 15 minutes

# ESSENTIAL PROVISIONS

## Food

1 kilogram/day*

↓

Fresh

24 hours+ on the trail?

Canned

Dehydrated

**May reduce food weight 60-90%**

Hot meal?

*assuming ~4 calories/gram

## Water

2-3 litres/day

↓

Unsafe drinking water?

Boil

Filter

Sterilise

Stove

Water filter

Chemical tablets (iodine/chlorine)

Pot & utensils

Fuel → Lighter/Matches

(!) Harmful microorganisms may be present in untreated water

## PACK WEIGHT GOAL
## 25%
## OF BODY WEIGHT OR LESS

 Handy tip

? Consideration

(!) Warning

# Malaria: ● Risk ● Cause ● Prevention

## Malaria risk around the world

● Countries where malaria transmission occurs
● Countries with limited risk of malaria transmission

**247m cases of malaria per year**

Africa: 212 million (86%)
Asia: 21 million (9%)
Middle East: 8.1 million (3%)
Americas: 2.7 million (1%)

**Number of countries affected**

109 countries. 30 countries in Sub-Saharan Africa and 5 in Asia account for 98% of global malaria deaths.

**881,000 deaths from malaria per year**

Africa: 801,000 (90.9%)
Middle East: 38,000 (4.1%)
Asia: 36,000 (4%)
Americas: 3,000 (0.3%)

**47.2%**

## Top five countries with most malaria transmissions

These account for 47.2% of total cases in the world each year

1. Nigeria: 57,506,000 (23.3%)
2. Democratic Republic of the Congo: 23,620,000 (9.6%)
3. Ethiopia: 12,405,000 (5%)
4. United Republic of Tanzania: 11,540,000 (4.7%)
5. Kenya: 11,342,000 (4.6%)

## Main cause of infection

Malaria is mainly spread by female anopheles mosquitoes. If a mosquito bites a person infected with malaria, it can then carry the parasite and spread it to other people after it has developed in the mosquito.

The adult female anopheles mosquito lives for, on average, about 2 weeks and will produce anywhere from 1,000 to 3,000 eggs throughout her lifetime.

### Population at risk
3.3 billion (half of the world population)

**85%** of deaths are children under 5 years old

An estimated **35%** of children in malaria-endemic countries slept under a net in 2010

## Malaria is a preventable infection that can be fatal if left untreated

Malaria can be avoided by following the simple ABCD of malaria treatment

**A** **Aware:** Research the country you are visiting

**B** **Bites:** Avoid mosquito bites by taking appropriate measures

**C** **Chemoprophylaxis:** Take anti-malarial medication exactly as prescribed

**D** **Diagnosis:** Prompt diagnosis and treatment

### Insecticide-treated nets delivered by manufacturers to countries in sub-Saharan Africa, 2010

Nigeria: 30 million (27.3%)
Ethiopia: 25 million (22.7%)
DR Congo: 10 million (9.1%)
UR Tanzania: 5 million (4.5%)
Kenya: 5 million (4.5%)
All other countries: 35 million (31.9%)

Sources: who.int, rollbackmalaria.org, traveldoctor.co.uk

# UNESCO & TOURISM

Unesco has been identifying **World Heritage Sites** since 1972, and today there are 911 sites on its list. Let's see where these significant places are, and compare their locations to the percentages of tourists who visit those countries.

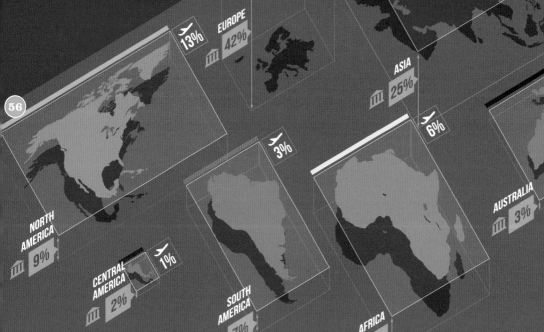

53%

23%

13%

**EUROPE**
42%

**ASIA**
25%

1%

6%

**NORTH AMERICA**
9%

3%

**AUSTRALIA**
3%

**CENTRAL AMERICA**
2%

1%

**SOUTH AMERICA**
7%

**AFRICA**
12%

56

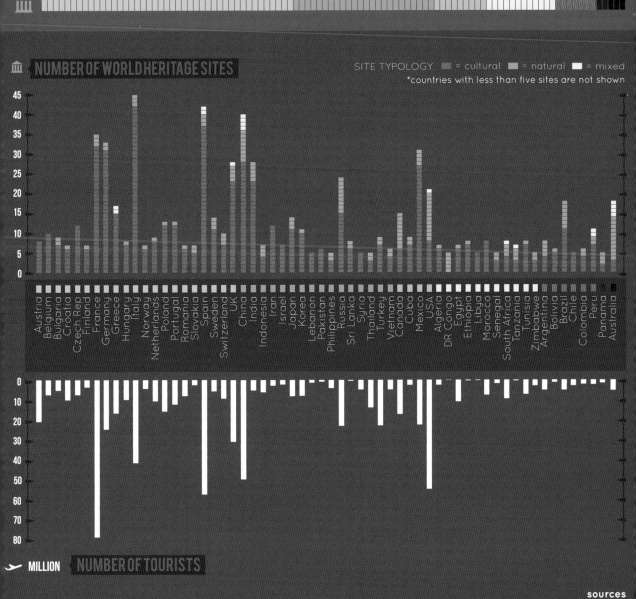

## NUMBER OF WORLD HERITAGE SITES

SITE TYPOLOGY ▮ = cultural ▮ = natural ▮ = mixed
*countries with less than five sites are not shown

45
40
35
30
25
20
15
10
5
0

Austria, Belgium, Bulgaria, Croatia, Czech Rep, Finland, France, Germany, Greece, Hungary, Italy, Norway, Netherlands, Poland, Portugal, Romania, Slovakia, Spain, Sweden, Switzerland, UK, China, India, Iran, Indonesia, Israel, Japan, Korea, Lebanon, Pakistan, Philippines, Russia, Sri Lanka, Syria, Thailand, Turkey, Vietnam, Canada, Cuba, Mexico, USA, Algeria, DR Congo, Egypt, Ethiopia, Libya, Morocco, Senegal, South Africa, Tanzania, Tunisia, Zimbabwe, Argentina, Bolivia, Brazil, Chile, Colombia, Peru, Panama, Australia

0
10
20
30
40
50
60
70
80

➤ MILLION   NUMBER OF TOURISTS

**sources**
Unesco data: *unesco.org*
Tourism data: *nationmaster.com + show.mappingworlds.com*

As of 2012, all flights into or out of the European Union will be subject to regulations that require airlines to buy carbon offsets to compensate for the greenhouse gases emitted by their aircraft. The airlines' costs will probably be passed along to passengers in the form of added fees. This infographic illustrates the additional cost (in euros and US dollars) for a one-way ticket to various destinations. Note, however, that estimates vary: the chart below shows emissions and costs as calculated by five different carbon-offset brokers.

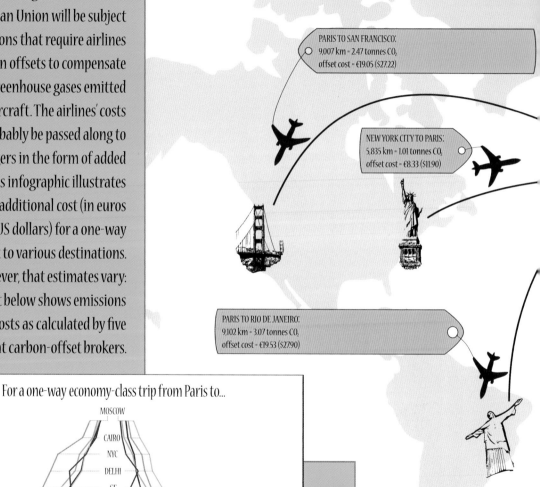

PARIS TO SAN FRANCISCO:
9,007 km = 2.47 tonnes CO₂
offset cost = €19.05 ($27.22)

NEW YORK CITY TO PARIS:
5,835 km = 1.01 tonnes CO₂
offset cost = €8.33 ($11.90)

PARIS TO RIO DE JANEIRO:
9,102 km = 3.07 tonnes CO₂
offset cost = €19.53 ($27.90)

For a one-way economy-class trip from Paris to...

MOSCOW
CAIRO
NYC
DELHI
SF
BEIJING
RIO
SYDNEY

6    5    4    3    2    1          15    30    45    60    75    90

CO₂ emissions per passenger (in tonnes)          cost of carbon offsets (in euros)

# THE COST OF CARBON OFFSETS

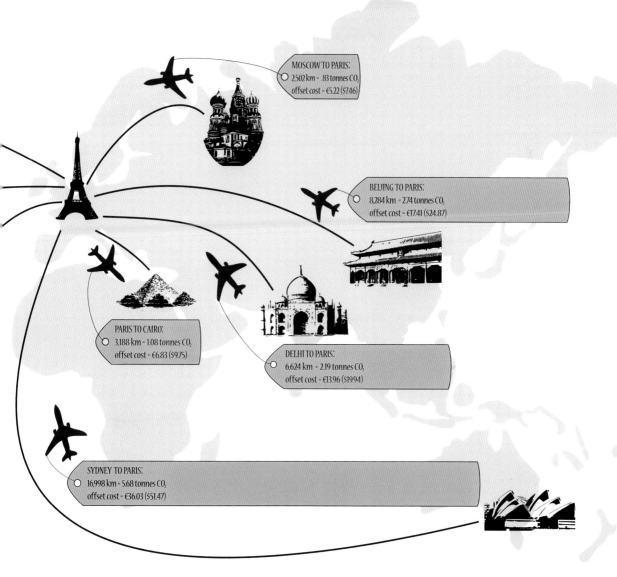

MOSCOW TO PARIS:
2,502 km = .83 tonnes CO$_2$
offset cost = €5.22 ($7.46)

BEIJING TO PARIS:
8,284 km = 2.74 tonnes CO$_2$
offset cost = €17.41 ($24.87)

PARIS TO CAIRO:
3,188 km = 1.08 tonnes CO$_2$
offset cost = €6.83 ($9.75)

DELHI TO PARIS:
6,624 km = 2.19 tonnes CO$_2$
offset cost = €13.96 ($19.94)

SYDNEY TO PARIS:
16,998 km = 5.68 tonnes CO$_2$
offset cost = €36.03 ($51.47)

Data pertain to one passenger on a one-way, economy class, nonstop flight. Figures and pricing are from calculators at carbonfund.org, carbonfootprint.com, carbonneutralcalculator.com, carbonplanet.com and terrapass.com. To ensure consistency, all calculations incorporate a Radiative Forcing Factor of 1.9, a figure recommended by the UK government agency DEFRA.

# WHERE TO RUN A MARATHON?
## SEVEN EXOTIC DESTINATIONS

BY CLARA & TINA

42.195KM

## WHERE DOES MARATHON COME FROM? (THE MYTH!)

Around 490BC, the story goes, a Greek soldier ran to Athens from the battlefield at Marathon, to announce their victory against the Persians – then collapsed and died from exhaustion.

## WANT SOMETHING NEW?

More than 500 marathons are contested throughout the world each year. World Marathon Majors are New York, Boston, Chicago, London and Berlin. If you have tried them all, why not pack your backpack and try one in a more exotic location?

## GETTING STARTED:

### THE TECHIE (RUNNER'S HIGH)

- HAIRBAND
- HEART–RATE MONITOR
- ENERGY BAR
- TECHNICAL RUNNING T–SHIRT
- LONG TIGHTS
- MINIMALIST RUNNING SHOES

### THE NEWBIE (HITTING THE WALL)

- SWEATING
- WATER
- COTTON T–SHIRT
- CAMERA
- MUSIC
- TRAINING SHOES

START!!

## FUN RECORDS:

In 2003 British adventurer Sir Ranulph Fiennes completed seven marathons on seven continents in seven days.

In 2010, Stefaan Engels, a Belgian, set out to run the marathon distance every day of the year. As of 5 February 2011, Engels had run 365 marathon distances in as many days.

## 1 ATHENS CLASSIC (THE OLDEST)

**WHERE & WHEN** Greece, November

**WHY** It's the home of the marathon!

## 7 ICE MARATHON (THE COLDEST)

**WHERE & WHEN** Antarctica, November

**WHY** Fancy racing against elephant seals and penguins in temperatures well below zero around glaciers and rocky beaches, with snow threatening to come down and cover the course throughout?

ALMOST THERE!

## 6 THE BIG FIVE MARATHON (THE WILDEST)

**WHERE & WHEN** South Africa, June

**WHY** Run with the BIG FIVE animals. No fences, no rivers, nothing at all separates you from the African wildlife. Armed rangers patrol the route to protect you!

ELEPHANT RHINO RUN FASTER!! BUFFALO LION LEOPARD

## 5 EVEREST MARATHON (THE HIGHEST)

**WHERE & WHEN** Nepal, December

**WHY** Listed in the Guinness Book of Records as the highest marathon in the world, it's also a contender for the world's most spectacular race.

3500FT!!

## 4 EGYPTIAN MARATHON (THE MYSTERIOUSEST)

**WHERE & WHEN** Egypt, January

**WHY** Not many people have completed this race under the ancient monuments. Want to give yourself a little challenge?

WAIT...

## 3 MARATHON DU MEDOU BORDEAUX (THE FUNNIEST)

**WHERE & WHEN** France, September

**WHY** What's better than passing through 53 vineyards with a bellyfull of wine and foie gras? C'est la vie! Three-quarters of the runners opt for fancy dress too.

TCHIN–TCHIN!

## 2 GREAT WALL MARATHON (THE HILLIEST)

**WHERE & WHEN** China, May

**WHY** Running on something as awe-inspiring and ancient as the Great Wall of China, 5,164 steps doesn't sound like too much.

加油！

# FAST FOOD, FAST FACTS

(FACTS FOUND AS PART OF INDEPENDENT INTERNET RESEARCH COMPLETED IN 2011, NOT STATISTICS OFFICIALLY SUPPLIED BY MCDONALD'S.)

  **#1** THE BUSIEST MCDONALD'S IN THE WORLD IS LOCATED IN PUSHKIN SQUARE, MOSCOW, SERVING OVER 40,000 CUSTOMERS EACH DAY.

  **#2** MCDONALD'S OFFERS A DELIVERY SERVICE IN 18 COUNTRIES, THREE OF WHICH PROVIDE 24-HOUR DELIVERY.

  **#3** ONLY 12 COUNTRIES, OUT OF THE 124 IN WHICH MCDONALD'S IS PRESENT, CURRENTLY SERVE ALCOHOL.

  **#4** BURGERS ARE BARBEQUED, NOT FRIED, IN TWO MCDONALD'S-SERVING COUNTRIES: ARGENTINA AND ISRAEL.

  **#5** THE SHEWSBURY MCDONALD'S IS THE OLDEST BUILDING TO HOUSE A MCDONALD'S RESTAURANT, DATING BACK TO THE 13TH CENTURY.

  **#6** THE WORLD'S FIRST SKI-THROUGH MCDONALD'S IS LOCATED IN SALEN, SWEDEN.

  **#7** THE INFOGRAPHIC BELOW PRESENTS SOME OF THE CHEAPEST, AND MOST EXPENSIVE, BIG MACS IN THE WORLD. (ALL LOCAL CURRENCIES CONVERTED TO USD.)

**$1.96**

**SRI LANKA**

**$1.91**

**HONG KONG**

**$1.80**

**UKRAINE**

$6.96

SWITZERLAND

$7.61

SWEDEN

$8.06

NORWAY

# ANATOMY *of a* WELL-PACKED BAG

Travelling is made so much easier with a small, well-packed bag. You can fit it under the seat of a bus, swing it over your front when on motorbikes and rickshaws, avoid baggage check-ins on flights and be happy walking around all day with it.

But there are many things to take into consideration, which can make the whole business daunting for the first-time backpacker. How much to take? To fold, roll or stuff? How do you minimise the chances of being robbed? What are the essential items?

Of course, the climate and style of travel will affect your packing list, but these tips aim to be as universal as possible.

### TIP 2 — SLEEPING SOUNDLY

A sleeping bag liner is much more portable than a full sleeping bag but will still protect you from those slightly questionable hostel sheets. Go for silk over cotton for coolness in the heat and warmth in the cold.

### TIP 1 — THE ART OF LAYERING

Clothes can be easily washed and dried so only take one item of every length of clothing – that way you can easily layer up if it's cold.

### TIP 4 — FEATHER-LIGHT FOOTSTEPS

Keep bulky footwear on your feet when moving around and pack some lightweight, more compact footwear.

### TIP 3 — DAYTIME TRAVELS

Take a separate easy-to-fold shoulder bag that you can take out on daytrips.

Wrap loo roll around the lids of toiletries and place inside a plastic bag to avoid messy accidents.

**FRONT OUTSIDE POCKET**

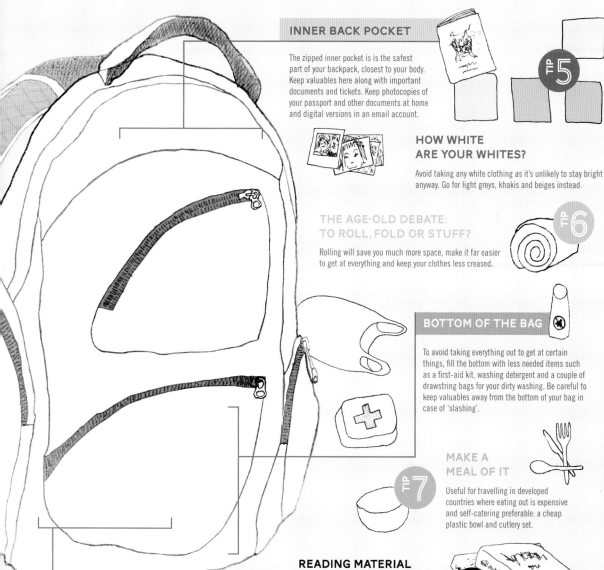

## INNER BACK POCKET

The zipped inner pocket is is the safest part of your backpack, closest to your body. Keep valuables here along with important documents and tickets. Keep photocopies of your passport and other documents at home and digital versions in an email account.

TIP 5

## HOW WHITE ARE YOUR WHITES?

Avoid taking any white clothing as it's unlikely to stay bright anyway. Go for light greys, khakis and beiges instead.

## THE AGE-OLD DEBATE: TO ROLL, FOLD OR STUFF?

Rolling will save you much more space, make it far easier to get at everything and keep your clothes less creased.

TIP 6

## BOTTOM OF THE BAG

To avoid taking everything out to get at certain things, fill the bottom with less needed items such as a first-aid kit, washing detergent and a couple of drawstring bags for your dirty washing. Be careful to keep valuables away from the bottom of your bag in case of 'slashing'.

## MAKE A MEAL OF IT

TIP 7

Useful for travelling in developed countries where eating out is expensive and self-catering preferable: a cheap plastic bowl and cutlery set.

## READING MATERIAL

Take just one or two paperbacks and when you're finished with them, swap for other books people have left in hostels and cafes.

TIP 8

Sources: **Jess Perriam** (twitter.com/jessyp) / **Travel Independent** (travelindependent.info)

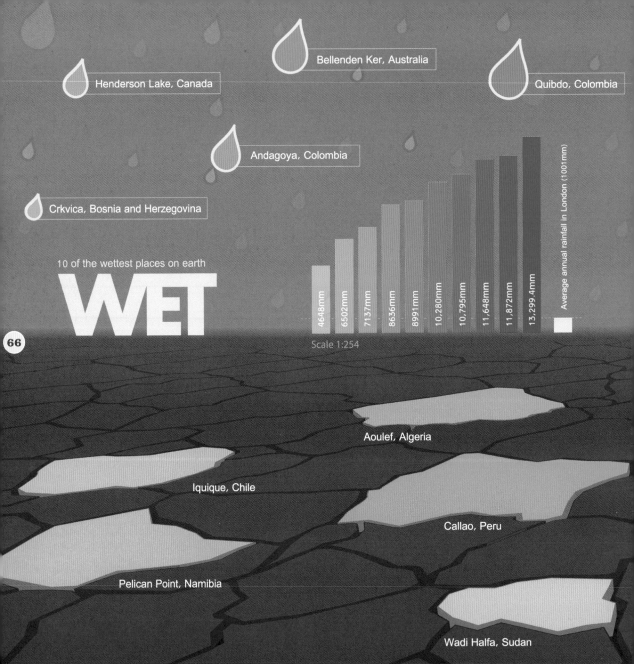

Henderson Lake, Canada

Bellenden Ker, Australia

Quibdo, Colombia

Andagoya, Colombia

Crkvica, Bosnia and Herzegovina

10 of the wettest places on earth

# WET

4648mm
6502mm
7137mm
8636mm
8991mm
10,280mm
10,795mm
11,648mm
11,872mm
13,299.4mm

Average annual rainfall in London (1001mm)

Scale 1:254

Aoulef, Algeria

Iquique, Chile

Callao, Peru

Pelican Point, Namibia

Wadi Halfa, Sudan

Debundscha, Cameroon

Mt Waialeale, Hawaii, USA

Lloro, Colombia

Cherrapunji, India

Mawsynram, India

Scale 1:1

12.191mm
12.19mm
8.3mm
5.08mm
2.54mm
2.29mm
0.862mm
0.861mm
0.86mm
0.76mm

# DRY
10 of the driest places on earth

Al Kufrah, Libya

Arica, Chile

Ica, Peru

Luxor, Egypt

Aswan, Egypt

Sources: wikipedia.org, thetravelalmanac.com, aneki.com

## SHARP OBJECTS

**●● SCISSORS**
In carry-on bags, metal scissors with pointed tips and blades shorter than 4" allowed

**● RAZOR-TYPE BLADES**
Including box cutters, utility knives and safety razor blades (plus disposable razors)

**● KNIVES & MEAT CLEAVERS**
Plastic or round-bladed butter knives allowed in carry-on bags

**● SWORDS & SABERS**
Cutting or thrusting weapons, including fencing foils

**● ICE PICKS & ICE AXES**

**NOTE** //////////////////////////
To prevent injury to baggage handlers and inspectors, sharp objects must be sheathed or securely wrapped

# BANNED

Remove all doubt about what you can and can't take with you on your next trip with this visual map of items banned for travel by the TSA.

*For detailed information, visit www.tsa.gov.*

## FLAMMABLE

⊘ BLASTING CAPS, DYNAMITE & FIREWORKS

⊘ HAND GRENADES & PLASTIC EXPLOSIVES
Realistic replicas of explosives are also banned

⊘ AEROSOLS
Limited quantities allowed for personal care or toiletries

⊘ FUELS & GASOLINE
Including any flammable liquid fuel and fuels used in cooking

⊘ GAS TORCHES

⊘ LIGHTER FLUID
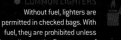

**68**

● COMMON LIGHTERS
Without fuel, lighters are permitted in checked bags. With fuel, they are prohibited unless they adhere to the Department of Transportation (DOT) exemption, which allows up to two fueled lighters if properly enclosed in a DOT approved case.

⊘ TORCH LIGHTERS
Their needle-like flame is more intense than common lighters (reaching 2,500° F)

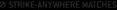

⊘ STRIKE-ANYWHERE MATCHES
One book of safety matches (non-strike anywhere) is allowed in carry-on bags

⊘ FLAMMABLE PAINTS, TURPENTINE & PAINT THINNER

⊘ Some other items banned completely
Chlorine for pools and spas, fire extinguishers and other compressed gas cylinders, liquid bleach, spillable batteries (except those in wheelchairs), spray paint, tear gas, vehicle airbags

## TOOLS

**NOTE** /////////////
All tools greater than 7" in length will have to be put into checked baggage

**●● HATCHETS & AXES**

**●● CATTLE PRODS & CROWBARS**

**● HAMMERS**

**●● WRENCHES & PLIERS**

**●● SCREWDRIVERS**

**● DRILLS & SAWS**
Including cordless portable power saws, power drills and drill bits

 **BASEBALL & CRICKET BATS** ●

 **BOWS & ARROWS** ●

 **LACROSSE & HOCKEY STICKS** ●

**NOTE** ////////////////////
Baseballs, soccer balls and basketballs can go through the passenger security checkpoint

 **DUMBBELLS** ●
[Hand weights]

 **GOLF CLUBS & POOL CUES** ●

**SKI POLES** ●

# SPORTS OBJECTS

 **BB GUNS & PELLET GUNS** ●

 **COMPRESSED AIR GUNS** ●
[Including paintball markers]
In checked luggage without compressed air cylinder

 **FLARE GUNS** * ●

 **FLARES** ⊘

 **GUN LIGHTERS** ●
Permitted only if it does not contain lighter fluid

 **GUN POWDER** ⊘
Including black powder and percussion caps

 **REALISTIC REPLICAS OF FIREARMS** ●

 **STARTER PISTOLS** * ●

## KEY

● Take in carry-on bag
● Take in checked bag
⊘ Not allowed to carry

# FIREARMS

* MUST be unloaded, packed in a locked hard-sided container, and declared to the airline at check-in

# SELF-DEFENSE/MARTIAL ARTS

 **BILLY CLUBS, BLACK JACKS & NIGHT STICKS** ●

 **BRASS KNUCKLES, THROWING STARS** ●

 **KUBATONS** ●

 **SELF-DEFENSE SPRAYS** ●

 **NUNCHAKUS** ●

 **STUN GUNS** ●
[Shocking devices]

## TOP 5 *weirdest* ITEMS EVER CONFISCATED

### 1 / SNAKES
A woman was arrested attempting to smuggle 75 live snakes inside her bra in Stockholm, Sweden.

### 2 / TROPICAL FISH
A woman in Melbourne, Australia, was nabbed attempting to import 51 live tropical fish in an apron of water-filled bags beneath her skirt.

### 3 / HUMAN EYEBALLS
A passenger in the UK was caught carrying a jam jar filled with 10 human eyeballs.

### 4 / GECKOS & PYTHONS
A man was found in the town of Kristiansand with packages strapped to his legs, altogether holding 10 albino leopard geckos and 14 royal pythons.

### 5 / RARE BIRDS
A man in Los Angeles smuggled four rare birds of paradise in his suitcase — discovered when they escaped and flew through the terminal. He also had two endangered slow loris pygmy monkeys hidden in his underwear.

SOURCE: WWW.TELEGRAPH.CO.UK

## WHAT HAPPENS TO CONFISCATED ITEMS?

Since the FAA doesn't have a policy about what's done with confiscated personal items, the procedure for dealing with them varies in every airport. Mostly they are thrown away, destroyed or donated to charities. Of late, several states are making a good profit by auctioning the items on sites like eBay.

SOURCE: WWW.CBSNEWS.COM

# A Lonely Planet

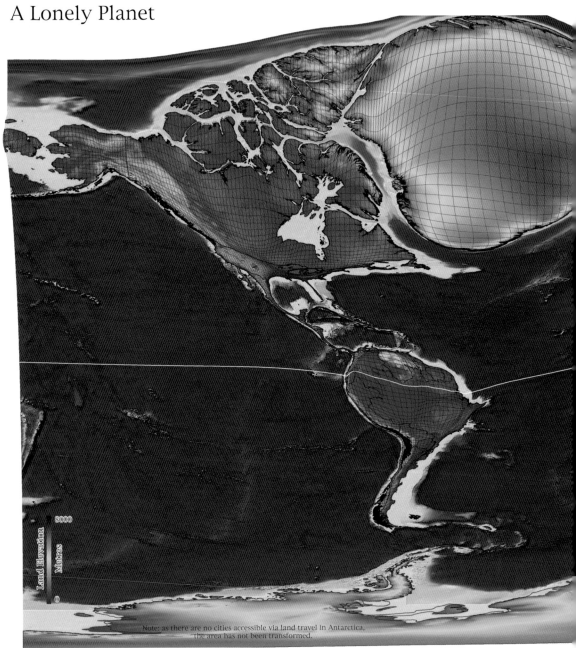

Land Elevation
Metres

8000

0

Note: as there are no cities accessible via land travel in Antarctica, the area has not been transformed.

**Data Sources** Global Topographic and Bathymetric Data: US Geological Survey (USGS); Accessibility Data: Global Environment Monitoring Unit – Joint Resea

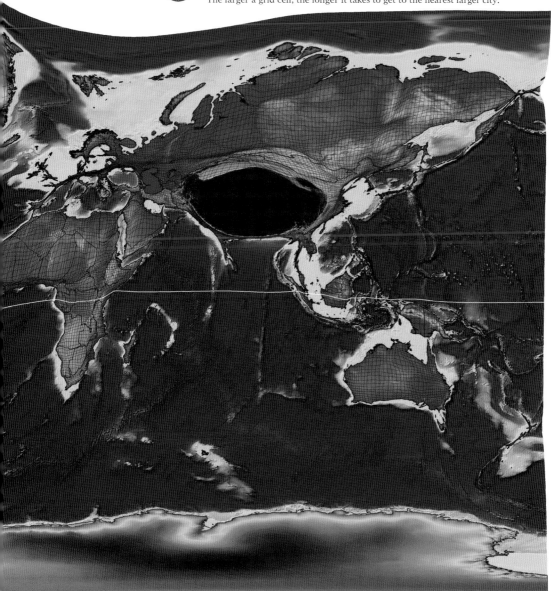

# A map showing the remotest spots in the world

Each grid cell on the map is related to the same amount of space in the physical world. The size of a grid cell reflects its accessibility, as measured by the time it takes to travel to the nearest city (with a population of 50,000+) over land. The larger a grid cell, the longer it takes to get to the nearest larger city.

of the European Commission, Ispra, Italy.

# MICROTRAVEL IN A
# **MICROWORLD**

Often dismissed as being eccentric or ephemeral, micronations are entities that make the claim of being an independent nation when they're actually not recognized by any existing government. More often than not they are founded by a single person or family group, and end up existing only on paper, on the internet, or in the minds of their founders.

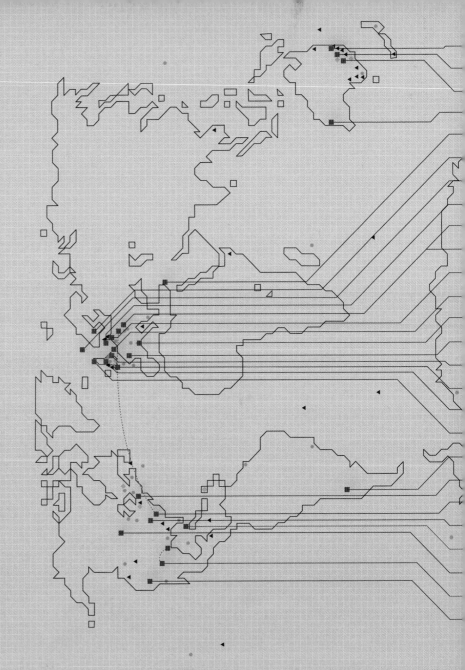

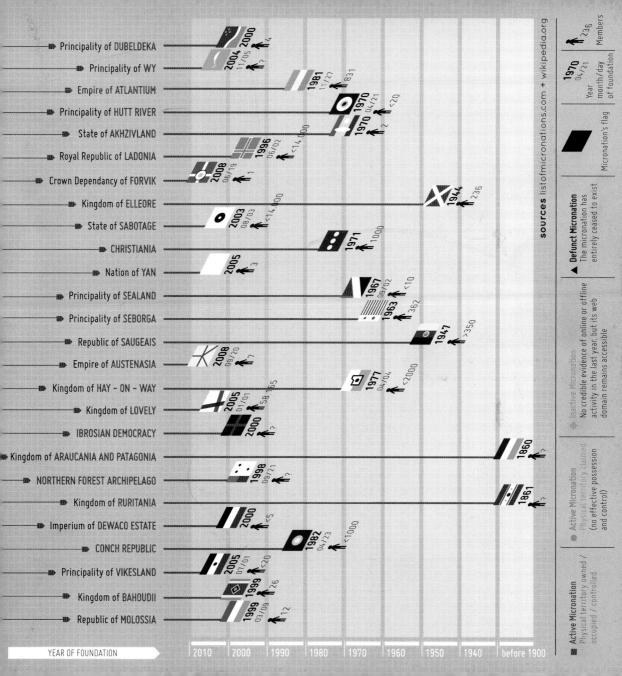

Principality of DUBELDEKA · 2000 · 11/05 · ↟4
Principality of WY · 2004 · 11/05 · ↟?
Empire of ATLANTIUM · 1981 · 11/27 · ↟831
Principality of HUTT RIVER · 1970 · 04/21 · ↟<20
State of AKHZIVLAND · 1970 · ↟2
Royal Republic of LADONIA · 1996 · 06/02 · ↟<14,000
Crown Dependancy of FORVIK · 2008 · 06/10 · ↟1
Kingdom of ELLEORE · 1944 · ↟236
State of SABOTAGE · 2003 · 08/03 · ↟<14,000
CHRISTIANIA · 1971 · ↟1000
Nation of YAN · 2005 · ↟3
Principality of SEALAND · 1967 · 09/02 · ↟<10
Principality of SEBORGA · 1963 · ↟362
Republic of SAUGEAIS · 1947 · ↟>350
Empire of AUSTENASIA · 2008 · 09/20 · ↟7
Kingdom of HAY – ON – WAY · 1977 · 04/01 · ↟<2000
Kingdom of LOVELY · 2005 · 01/01 · ↟58,465
IBROSIAN DEMOCRACY · 2000 · ↟?
Kingdom of ARAUCANIA AND PATAGONIA · 1860 · ↟?
NORTHERN FOREST ARCHIPELAGO · 1998 · 09/21 · ↟?
Kingdom of RURITANIA · 1861 · ↟?
Imperium of DEWACO ESTATE · 2000 · ↟<5
CONCH REPUBLIC · 1982 · 04/23 · ↟<1000
Principality of VIKESLAND · 2005 · 07/01 · ↟<20
Kingdom of BAHOUDII · 1999 · ↟26
Republic of MOLOSSIA · 1999 · 03/09 · ↟12

YEAR OF FOUNDATION

2010 · 2000 · 1990 · 1980 · 1970 · 1960 · 1950 · 1940 · before 1900

sources listofmicronations.com + wikipedia.org

1970 · 04/21 · Year month/day of foundation
↟236 Members
Micronation's flag

▲ **Defunct Micronation** The micronation has entirely ceased to exist

◆ Inactive Micronation No credible evidence of online or offline activity in the last year, but its web domain remains accessible

● **Active Micronation** Physical territory claimed (no effective possession and control)

⚑ **Active Micronation** Physical territory owned / occupied / controlled

# ANTIPODEAN GETAWAYS

Plan your biggest trip yet! Just find the city closest to you and follow the flight path to the antipodean airport. You could end up travelling anywhere from 17,000km (Nuuk to Stewart Island) to 19,500km (Barcelona to Chatham Islands) to reach your next greatest adventure. What's your destination?

CITY, Country | AIRPORT CODE | Currency

- APIA, Samoa | APW | Tālā
- NAPUKA, French Polynesia | NAU | Pacifique Franc
- CAPE TOWN, South Africa | CPT | Rand
- CHATHAM ISLANDS, New Zealand | CHT | NZ Dollar
- TAHITI, French Polynesia | PPT | Pacifique Franc
- NADI, Republic of Fiji | NAN | Fiji Dollar
- LIMA, Peru | LIM | Nuevo Sol
- CHATHAM ISLANDS, New Zealand | CHT | NZ Dollar
- CHATHAM ISLANDS, New Zealand | CHT | NZ Dollar
- JAKARTA, Indonesia | CGK | Rupiah
- TAIPEI, Taiwan | TPE | Taiwanese New Dollar
- CHATHAM ISLANDS, New Zealand | CHT | NZ Dollar
- CHATHAM ISLANDS, New Zealand | CHT | NZ Dollar
- XUZHOU, China | XUZ | Yuan Renminbi
- TAHITI, French Polynesia | PPT | Pacifique Franc
- MALANG, Indonesia | MLG | Rupiah
- NEW PLYMOUTH, New Zealand | NPL | Rupiah
- TOLANARO, Madagascar | FTU | Ariary
- PORT VILA, Vanuatu | VLI | Vatu
- NUKU, French Polynesia | NHV | Pacifique Franc
- EASTER ISLAND, Chile | IPC | Chilean Peso
- LA SERENA, Chile | LSC | Chilean Peso
- HAGÅTÑA, Guam | GUM | US Dollar
- MEDAN, Indonesia | MES | Rupiah
- ANTOFAGASTA, Chile | ANF | Chilean Peso
- GERALDTON, Australia | GET | Australian Dollar
- SAN SALVADOR DE JUJUY, Argentina | ZSA | Argentine Peso
- TOLANARO, Madagascar | FTU | Ariary
- TAHITI, French Polynesia | PPT | Pacifique Franc
- BOGOTA, Colombia | BOG | Colombian Peso
- BORA BORA, French Polynesia | BOB | Pacifique Franc
- APIA, Samoa | APW | Tālā
- EASTER ISLAND, Chile | IPC | Chilean Peso
- MATAIVA, French Polynesia | MVT | Pacifique Franc

Currency | AIRPORT CODE | Country, CITY

- African Franc | ABJ | Ivory Coast, ABIDJAN
- Birr | ADD | Ethiopia, ADDIS ABABA
- US Dollar | ANC | USA, ANCHORAGE
- Euro | ATH | Greece, ATHENS
- Dinar | BGW | Iraq, BAGHDAD
- Manat | GYD | Azerbaijan, BAKU
- African Franc | BKO | Mali, BAMAKO
- Bhat | BKK | Thailand, BANGKOK
- Euro | BCN | Spain, BARCELONA
- Euro | TXL | Germany, BERLIN
- Colombian Peso | BOG | Colombia, BOGOTA
- Reais | BSB | Brazil, BRASILIA
- Lei | OTP | Romania, BUCHAREST
- Forint | BUD | Hungary, BUDAPEST
- Peso | EZE | Argentina, BUENOS AIRES
- Egyptian Pound | CAI | Egypt, CAIRO
- Rand | CPT | South Africa, CAPE TOWN
- Bolívar Fuerte | CCS | Venezuela, CARACAS
- Dirhams | CMN | Morocco, CASABLANCA
- US Dollar | ORD | USA, CHICAGO
- African Franc | DKR | Senegal, DAKAR
- Tanzanian Shilling | DAR | Tanzania, DAR ES SALAAM
- Pakistani Rupee | DEL | India, DELHI
- Taka | DAC | Bangladesh, DHAKA
- Real | FOR | Brazil, FORTALEZA
- US Dollar | GYE | Ecuador, GUAYAQUIL
- Dong | HAN | Vietnam, HANOI
- Zimbabwean Dollar | HRE | Zimbabwe, HARARE
- Convertible Peso | HAV | Cuba, HAVANA
- Hong Kong Dollar | HKG | China, HONG KONG
- US Dollar | IAH | USA, HOUSTON
- Lira | IST | Turkey, ISTANBUL
- Rupiah | CGK | Indonesia, JAKARTA
- Ugandan Shilling | KLA | Uganda, KAMPALA
- Naira | KAN | Nigeria, KANO
- Pakistani Rupee | KHI | Pakistan, KARACHI
- Sudanese Pound | KRT | Sudan, KHARTOUM

NEW PLYMOUTH, New Zealand | NPL | NZ Dollar
CHATHAM ISLANDS, New Zealand | CHT | NZ Dollar
PORT ELIZABETH, South Africa | PLZ | Rand
HILO, Hawaii | ITO | US Dollar
HILO, Hawaii | ITO | US Dollar
SANDAKAN, Malaysia | SDK | Ringgit
CUIABA, Brazil | CGB | Real
HILO, Hawaii | ITO | US Dollar
PORT LOUIS, Mauritius | MRU | Mauritian Rupee
CHATHAM ISLANDS, New Zealand | CHT | NZ Dollar
HIVA OA, French Polynesia | HIX | Pacifique Franc
ALBANY, Australia | ALH | Australian Dollar
STEWART ISLAND, New Zealand | SZS | NZ Dollar
EASTER ISLAND, Chile | IPC | Chilean Peso
NUKU, French Polynesia | NHV | Pacifique Franc
TÔLANARO, Madagascar | FTU | Ariary
STEWART ISLAND, New Zealand | SZS | NZ Dollar
STEWART ISLAND, New Zealand | SZS | NZ Dollar
STEWART ISLAND, New Zealand | SZS | NZ Dollar
CHATHAM ISLANDS, New Zealand | CHT | NZ Dollar
XI'AN, China | XIY | Yuan Renminbi
TAIPEI, Taiwan | TPE | Taiwan New Dollar
MAR DEL PLATA, Argentina | MDQ | Argentine Peso
ROSARIO, Argentina | ROS | Argentine Peso
QUITO, Ecuador | UIO | US Dollar
STEWART ISLAND, New Zealand | SZS | NZ Dollar
CHATHAM ISLANDS, New Zealand | CHT | NZ Dollar
MADEIRA ISLAND, Portugal | FNC | Euro
TAHITI, French Polynesia | PPT | Pacifique Franc
MONTEVIDEO, Uruguay | MVD | Uruguayan Peso
MARGARET RIVER, Australia | MQZ | Australian Dollar
PUNTA ARENAS, Chile | PUQ | Chilean Peso
PORT ELIZABETH, South Africa | PLZ | Rand
CHATHAM ISLANDS, New Zealand | CHT | NZ Dollar
TÔLANARO, Madagascar | FTU | Ariary
APIA, Samoa | APW | Tālā

Euro | LIS | Portugal, LISBON
British Pound | LHR | United Kingdom, LONDON
Kwanza | LAD | Angola, LUANDA
Congolese Franc | FBM | Democratic Republic of the Congo, LUBUMBASHI
Philippine Peso | MNL | Philippines, MANILA
Real | MAO | Brazil, MANAUS
Metical | MPM | Mozambique, MAPUTO
Mexican Peso | MEX | Mexico, MEXICO CITY
Euro | MXP | Italy, MILAN
Somalian Shilling | MGQ | Somalia, MUQDISHO
Canadian Dollar | | Canada, MONTREAL
Ruble | DME | Russia, MOSCOW
Indian Rupee | BOM | India, MUMBAI
Kenyan Shilling | NBO | Kenya, NAIROBI
US Dollar | JFK | USA, NEW YORK
Krone | GOH | Greenland, NUUK
Euro | CDG | France, PARIS
Icelandic Króna | RKV | Iceland, REYKJAVIK
Euro | CIA | Italy, ROME
Chilean Peso | SCL | Chile, SANTIAGO
Real | GRU | Brazil, SÃO PAULO
Won | ICN | South Korea, SEOUL
Yuan Renminbi | SHA | China, SHANGHAI
Singapore Dollar | SIN | Singapore, SINGAPORE
Ruble | LED | Russia, ST. PETERSBURG
Swedish Krona | ARN | Sweden, STOCKHOLM
Australian Dollar | SYD | Australia, SYDNEY
Rial | IKA | Iran, TEHRAN
Yen | HND | Japan, TOKYO
Canadian Dollar | YYZ | Canada, TORONTO
Tugrik | ULN | Mongolia, ULAANBAATAR
Canadian Dollar | YVR | Canada, VANCOUVER
Zloty | WAW | Poland, WARSAW
Canadian Dollar | YWG | Canada, WINNIPEG
African Franc | YAO | Cameroon, YAOUNDE

Information is correct as of May 2011.

■ Africa  ■ North America  ■ South America  ■ Europe  ■ Oceania  ■ Asia

# GREAT RAILWAY JOURNEYS

## THE TRANS-SIBERIAN RAILWAY

**0000km**

## THE ORIENT EXPRESS

**PARIS** — **ISTANBUL**

$CO_2$ **377** kg

**Shared Suite** $17,230

119H 25M*

27* km/h

*includes overnight hotel stays*

**0000km** — **3186km**

## THE INDIAN PACIFIC

**SYDNEY** — **PERTH**

$CO_2$ **515** kg

**Gold Class Ticket** $2,109

70H 22M

61 km/h

**0000km** — **4352km**

## THE CANADIAN

**VANCOUVER** — **TORONTO**

$CO_2$ **528** kg

**1ST Class Ticket** $1,906

83H 08M

53 km/h

**0000km** — **4466km**

**VLADIVOSTOK**

CO₂ 1099 kg | 1st Class Ticket $1,685 | 146H 08M | 77 km/h

9288 km

# JINGHU HIGH SPEED RAIL

**BEIJING** **SHANGHAI**

CO₂ 154 kg | 1st Class Ticket $173* | 05H 00M | 260 km/h

*\* as of July 2011*

0000 km | 1303 km

# THE BLUE TRAIN

**PRETORIA** **CAPE TOWN**

CO₂ 189 kg | Gold Class Ticket $3,170 | 27H 10M | 57 km/h

0000 km | 1600 km

## SOURCES

**The Trans-Siberian Railway**:
www.lonelyplanet.com/russia/russian-far-east/vladivostok/travel-tips-and-articles/38105

**The Orient Express** :
www.orient-express.com/web/vsoe/journeys/4_121933.jsp

**The Indian Pacific**:
www.gsr.com.au/site/indian_pacific.jsp

**The Canadian**:
www.viarail.ca/en/trains/rockies-and-pacific/toronto-vancouver-canadian

**Jinghu High-Speed Railway**:
www.chtrak.com

**The Blue Train**:
www.bluetrain.co.za/routes.htm#ScheduledRoutes

**"CO₂ Emissions & Global Warming: Trains versus Planes"**: www.seat61.com/CO2flights.htm

## legend

**How Fast?**
Average speed in kilometres per hour

**Are we there yet?**
Travel time in hours and minutes

**Tickets please!**
Cost of single fare
(US$ as of May 2011)

**Carbon created**
118 grams of carbon dioxide are created for each kilometre travelled by rail

**PARIS**

**All aboard!**
Names of great cities at the start and end of each famous journey

**Distance**
Start and end markers show the distance travelled

1. Bangkok, Thailand (Try: Pad Thai)

2. Rome, Italy (Try: Pizza)

6. Singapore (Try: Chicken Rice)

7. Tokyo, Japan (Try: Sushi)

10. Florence, Italy (Try: Ribollita)

11. Kuala Lumpur, Malaysia (Try: Laksa)

12. New Dehli, India (Try: Tandoori)

**3.** Paris, France (Try: Pot-Au-Feu)

**2.** Hong Kong (Try: Dim Sum)

**5.** New York, USA (Try: Bagels)

**8.** Lima, Peru (Try: Ceviche)

**9.** Barcelona, Spain (Try: Paella)

We asked *lonely planet* Facebook® fans,
"If you could travel to any city for the food, where would you go?"

Bangkok | Rome | Paris | Hong Kong | New York | Singapore | Tokyo | Lima | Barcelona | Florence | Kuala Lumpur | New Delhi

Source: Andy Murdock, Lonely Planet blog: If you could travel to any city for the food... (http://inside-digital.blog.lonelyplanet.com/2011/03/26/if-you-could-travel-to-any-city-for-the-food)

# Cups of Tea a Day
## vs Life Satisfaction

LIFE SATISFACTION (RATED OUT OF 10)

8.5
8
7.5
7
6.5
6
5.5
5
4.5
4

| 0.7 | 0.7 | 1.1 | 1.1 | 1.3 | 1.5 | 1.5 |

Switzerland  Sweden  China  Chile  Germany  India  Netherlan

AVERAGE CUPS OF TEA A DAY, PER PERSON

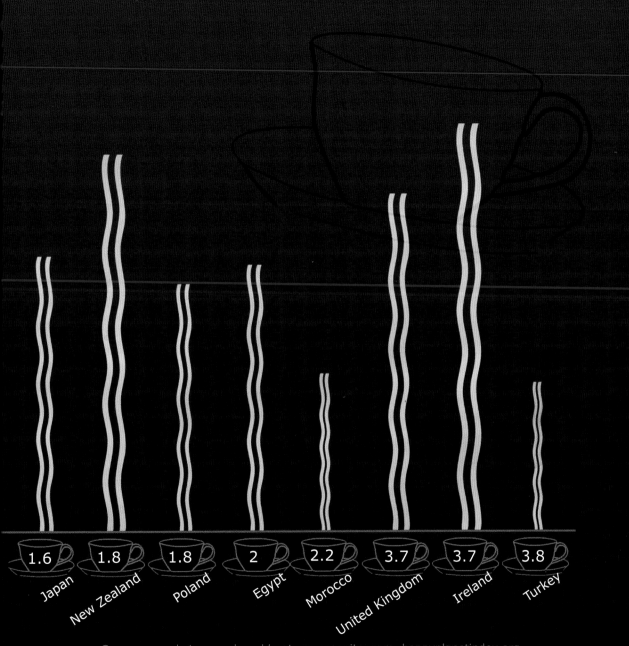

| 1.6 | 1.8 | 1.8 | 2 | 2.2 | 3.7 | 3.7 | 3.8 |
|-----|-----|-----|---|-----|-----|-----|-----|
| Japan | New Zealand | Poland | Egypt | Morocco | United Kingdom | Ireland | Turkey |

Sources: marketresearchworld.net, euromonitor.com, happyplanetindex.org

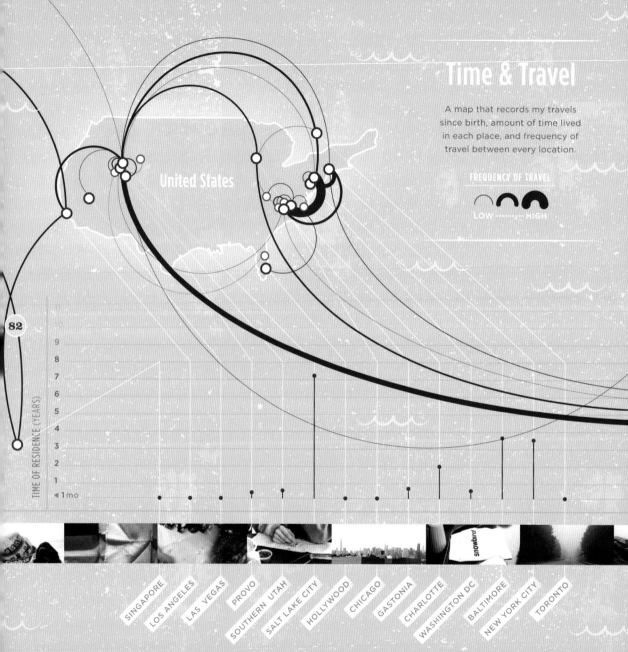

# Time & Travel

A map that records my travels since birth, amount of time lived in each place, and frequency of travel between every location.

**FREQUENCY OF TRAVEL**

LOW ·········· HIGH

United States

82

TIME OF RESIDENCE (YEARS)

9
8
7
6
5
4
3
2
1
◄ 1 mo

SINGAPORE
LOS ANGELES
LAS VEGAS
PROVO
SOUTHERN UTAH
SALT LAKE CITY
HOLLYWOOD
CHICAGO
GASTONIA
CHARLOTTE
WASHINGTON DC
BALTIMORE
NEW YORK CITY
TORONTO

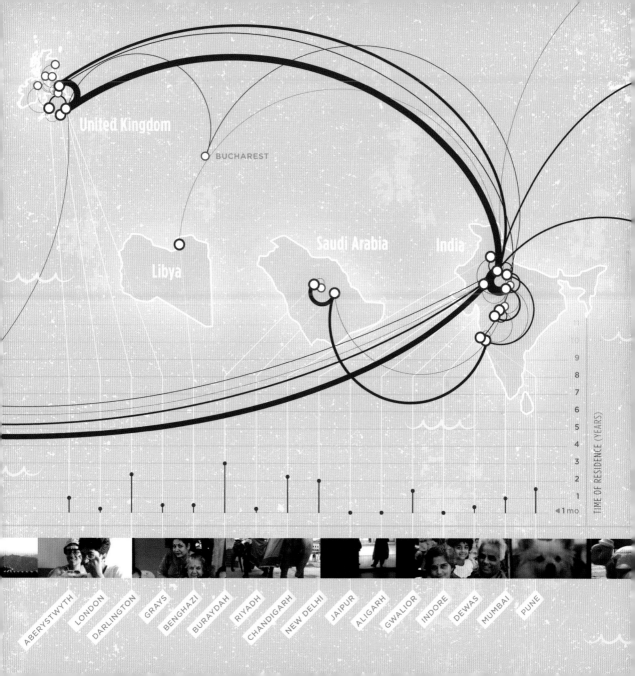

United Kingdom

BUCHAREST

Libya

Saudi Arabia

India

TIME OF RESIDENCE (YEARS)

10
9
8
7
6
5
4
3
2
1
◀1mo

ABERYSTWYTH  LONDON  DARLINGTON  GRAYS  BENGHAZI  BURAYDAH  RIYADH  CHANDIGARH  NEW DELHI  JAIPUR  ALIGARH  GWALIOR  INDORE  DEWAS  MUMBAI  PUNE

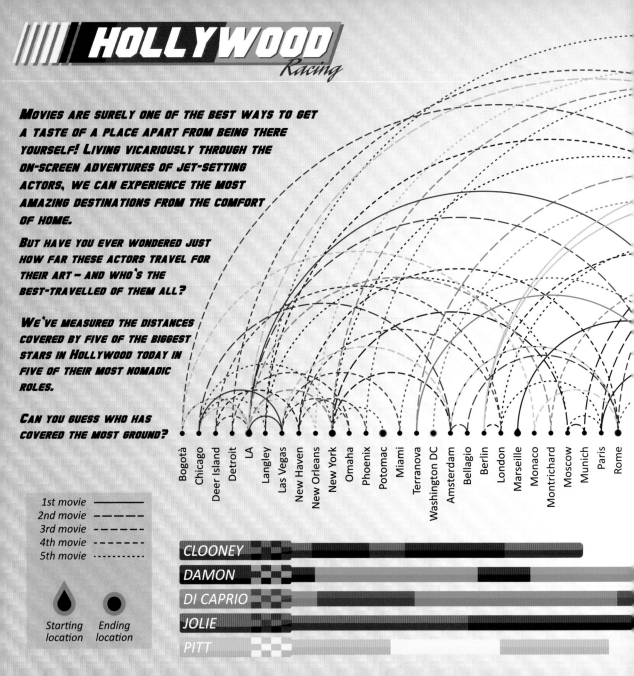

# HOLLYWOOD Racing

MOVIES ARE SURELY ONE OF THE BEST WAYS TO GET A TASTE OF A PLACE APART FROM BEING THERE YOURSELF! LIVING VICARIOUSLY THROUGH THE ON-SCREEN ADVENTURES OF JET-SETTING ACTORS, WE CAN EXPERIENCE THE MOST AMAZING DESTINATIONS FROM THE COMFORT OF HOME.

BUT HAVE YOU EVER WONDERED JUST HOW FAR THESE ACTORS TRAVEL FOR THEIR ART — AND WHO'S THE BEST-TRAVELLED OF THEM ALL?

WE'VE MEASURED THE DISTANCES COVERED BY FIVE OF THE BIGGEST STARS IN HOLLYWOOD TODAY IN FIVE OF THEIR MOST NOMADIC ROLES.

CAN YOU GUESS WHO HAS COVERED THE MOST GROUND?

Bogotà · Chicago · Deer Island · Detroit · LA · Langley · Las Vegas · New Haven · New Orleans · New York · Omaha · Phoenix · Potomac · Miami · Terranova · Washington DC · Amsterdam · Bellagio · Berlin · London · Marseille · Monaco · Montrichard · Moscow · Munich · Paris · Rome

1st movie ——
2nd movie – – –
3rd movie – – –
4th movie - - -
5th movie ·······

CLOONEY
DAMON
DI CAPRIO
JOLIE
PITT

Starting location · Ending location

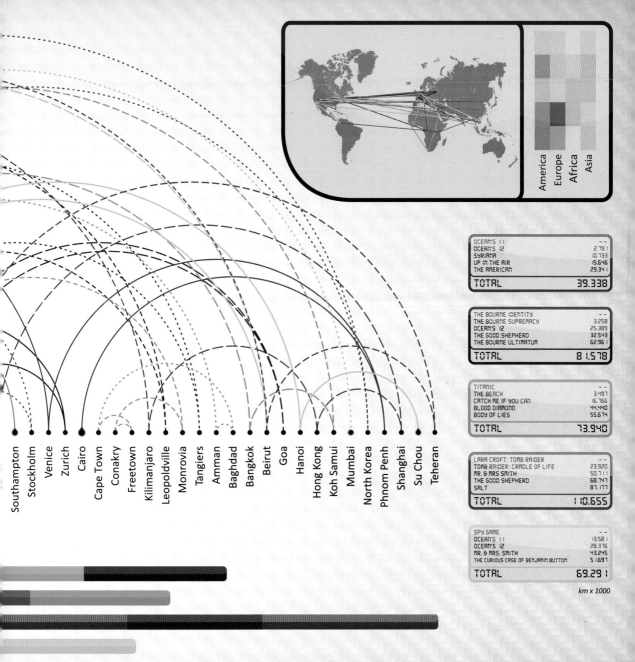

America · Europe · Africa · Asia

Southampton · Stockholm · Venice · Zurich · Cairo · Cape Town · Conakry · Freetown · Kilimanjaro · Leopoldville · Monrovia · Tangiers · Amman · Baghdad · Bangkok · Beirut · Goa · Hanoi · Hong Kong · Koh Samui · Mumbai · North Korea · Phnom Penh · Shanghai · Su Chou · Teheran

| OCEAN'S 11 | -- |
| OCEAN'S 12 | 2.791 |
| SYRIANA | 10.733 |
| UP IN THE AIR | 15.646 |
| THE AMERICAN | 29.341 |
| **TOTAL** | **39.338** |

| THE BOURNE IDENTITY | -- |
| THE BOURNE SUPREMACY | 3.258 |
| OCEAN'S 12 | 25.389 |
| THE GOOD SHEPHERD | 32.543 |
| THE BOURNE ULTIMATUM | 62.961 |
| **TOTAL** | **81.578** |

| TITANIC | -- |
| THE BEACH | 3.497 |
| CATCH ME IF YOU CAN | 16.766 |
| BLOOD DIAMOND | 44.440 |
| BODY OF LIES | 55.674 |
| **TOTAL** | **73.940** |

| LARA CROFT: TOMB RAIDER | -- |
| TOMB RAIDER: CRADLE OF LIFE | 23.920 |
| MR. & MRS. SMITH | 50.711 |
| THE GOOD SHEPHERD | 68.747 |
| SALT | 87.177 |
| **TOTAL** | **110.655** |

| SPY GAME | -- |
| OCEAN'S 11 | 13.581 |
| OCEAN'S 12 | 28.376 |
| MR. & MRS. SMITH | 43.245 |
| THE CURIOUS CASE OF BENJAMIN BUTTON | 51.697 |
| **TOTAL** | **69.291** |

km x 1000

sources: wikipedia.org, imdb.com

# LIFE AND DEATH ON THE ROAD

Road crashes are the leading cause of death among otherwise healthy travellers. This infographic looks at the rates of vehicle ownership and crash deaths (among all people, not just travellers) in the top 10 tourist destination countries.

Icons represent the vehicles owned per 200 population.
Red icons count the drivers and passengers who died in crashes, per 100,000 population.

🏍 🛺 Motorised 2-wheel and 3-wheel vehicles

🚗 🚗 Other motor vehicles

| Germany | United Kingdom | France | Italy |
|---|---|---|---|
| pop. 83m | pop. 61m | pop. 62m | pop. 59m |
| 4.6 deaths* | 4 deaths* | 6.3 deaths* | 7.2 deaths* |

In these 10 countries combined, someone dies in a road crash **every three minutes**.

| Spain | Turkey | China | United States | Mexico | Malaysia |
|-------|--------|-------|---------------|--------|----------|
| pop. 44m | pop. 75m | pop. 1.34b | pop. 306m | pop. 107m | pop. 27m |
| 7.5 deaths* | 8.4 deaths* | 8.4 deaths* | 11.5 deaths* | 15.2 deaths* | 19.2 deaths* |

* Motor vehicle driver and passenger deaths per 100,000 population that year. Does not include bicyclists or pedestrians.
Data is for 2007. Source: World Health Organization. Visualization by Damien Leri (bigyellowstar.com)

# Worldwide Crime Rates

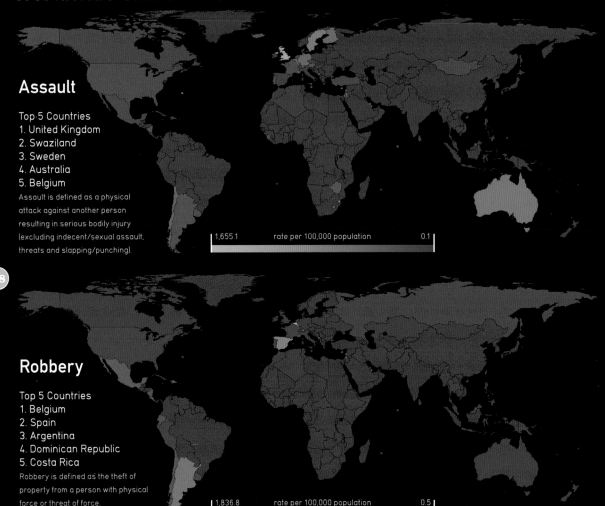

## Assault

Top 5 Countries
1. United Kingdom
2. Swaziland
3. Sweden
4. Australia
5. Belgium

Assault is defined as a physical
attack against another person
resulting in serious bodily injury
(excluding indecent/sexual assault,
threats and slapping/punching).

1,655.1          rate per 100,000 population          0.1

## Robbery

Top 5 Countries
1. Belgium
2. Spain
3. Argentina
4. Dominican Republic
5. Costa Rica

Robbery is defined as the theft of
property from a person with physical
force or threat of force.

1,836.8          rate per 100,000 population          0.5

Brighter countries have higher rates of specified crime per 100,000 people, based on recent data from the United Nations
Office on Drugs and Crime. Countries in grey had no applicable data.

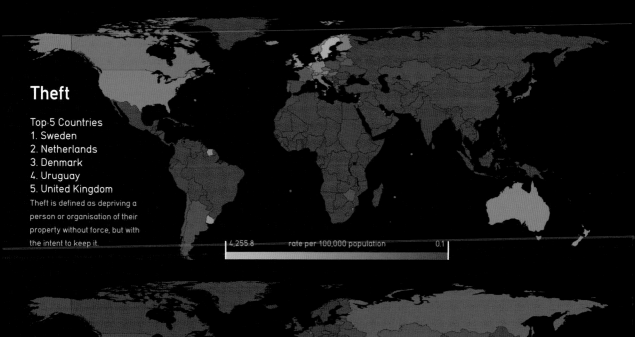

# Theft

Top 5 Countries
1. Sweden
2. Netherlands
3. Denmark
4. Uruguay
5. United Kingdom

Theft is defined as depriving a person or organisation of their property without force, but with the intent to keep it.

4,255.8        rate per 100,000 population        0.1

# Murder

Top 5 Countries
1. El Salvador
2. Honduras
3. Jamaica
4. Guatemala
5. Venezuela

Murder is defined as an unlawful death that is intentionally inflicted on a person by another person.

71        rate per 100,000 population        0

Source: www.unodc.org/unodc/en/data-and-analysis/crimedata.html

# Planet Holiday
## The world's major tourist destinations

The countries on this map are resized according to the
total number of tourist arrivals from other countries.

United Kingdom

United States
of America

Franc[e]

Mexico

Spain

## Top 10 Destinations

1. France
2. United States of America
3. Spain
4. China
5. Italy
6. United Kingdom
7. Turkey
8. Germany

10. Mexico

2009 International Tourist Arrivals
Using data from the World Bank
& the World Tourism Organization

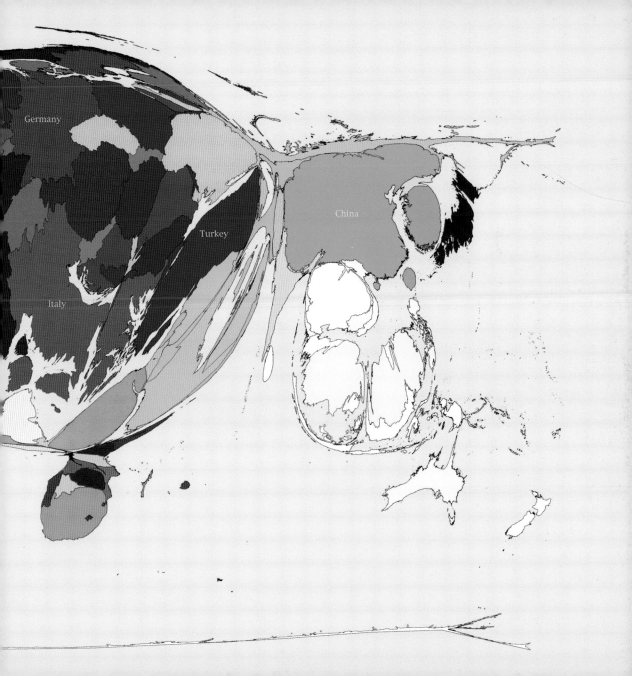

# Exploring the Unknown

Seeking fame, riches, adventure and knowledge, history's great travelers have crossed land, sea, air and space on their voyages of discovery.

Marco Polo
Italy
1271–1295

Vasco de Gama
Portugal
Jul. 8, 1497–Sep. 9, 1499

Charles Darwin
United Kingdom
Dec. 27, 1831–Oct. 2, 1836

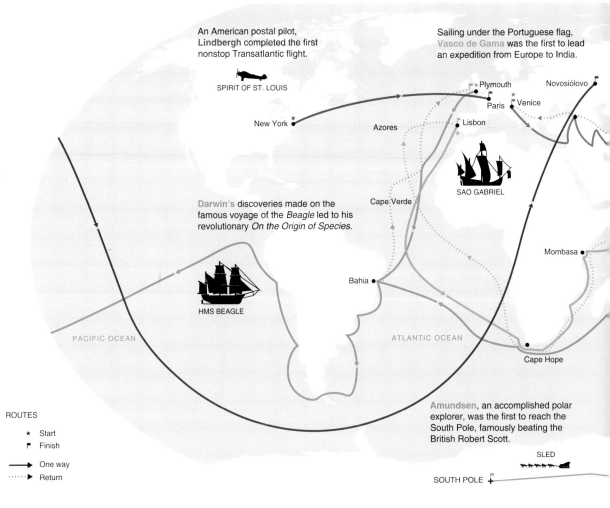

An American postal pilot, **Lindbergh** completed the first nonstop Transatlantic flight.

SPIRIT OF ST. LOUIS

Sailing under the Portuguese flag, **Vasco de Gama** was the first to lead an expedition from Europe to India.

New York

Azores

Plymouth
Paris    Venice
Lisbon

Novosiólovo

SAO GABRIEL

**Darwin's** discoveries made on the famous voyage of the *Beagle* led to his revolutionary *On the Origin of Species*.

Cape Verde

HMS BEAGLE

Bahia

Mombasa

PACIFIC OCEAN

ATLANTIC OCEAN

Cape Hope

**Amundsen**, an accomplished polar explorer, was the first to reach the South Pole, famously beating the British Robert Scott.

SLED

ROUTES

★   Start
⚑   Finish
→   One way
······▶   Return

SOUTH POLE

Roald Amundsen
Norway
Dec. 14, 1911–Jan. 25, 1912

Charles A. Lindbergh
USA
May 20, 1927–May 21, 1927

Yuri Gagarin
USSR
April 12, 1961 (6:07–7:55)

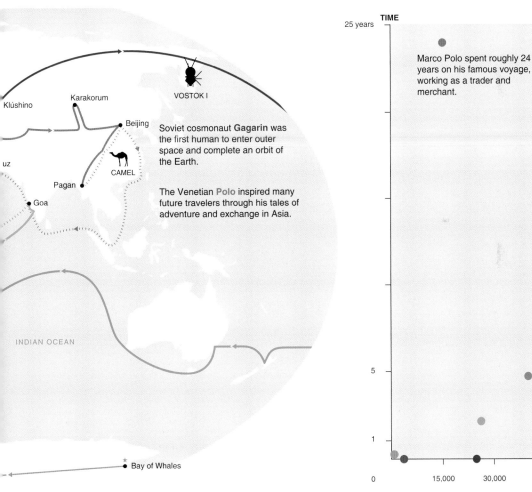

Klúshino

Karakorum

VOSTOK I

Beijing

uz

CAMEL

Pagan

Goa

Soviet cosmonaut **Gagarin** was the first human to enter outer space and complete an orbit of the Earth.

The Venetian **Polo** inspired many future travelers through his tales of adventure and exchange in Asia.

INDIAN OCEAN

Bay of Whales

TIME

25 years

Marco Polo spent roughly 24 years on his famous voyage, working as a trader and merchant.

5

1

DISTANCE

0          15,000          30,000          45,000 miles

# WORLD'S Largest ROADSIDE Attractions

*The Big Banana*
Coffs Harbour, New South Wales, Australia
World's Largest Banana
13m long x 5m high x 2.4m wide

## What is a large attraction?

To quote David Clark: "A big thing must be artificially made and it must be bigger than the real thing it represents."

There are

 **400** large roadside attractions in the world

94

 **66%**

Are found in the USA

Just over

 **12%**

are found in the southern hemisphere

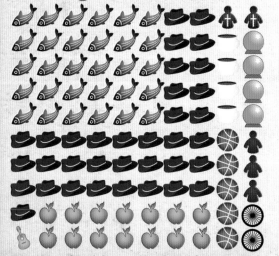

## The Big Breakdown:

 ● Animals     ● Sports

 ● Objects     ● People

 ● Food     ● Transport

 ● Mystical     ● Religious

 ● Drinks     ● Music

Percentage breakdown of roadside attractions

# Where you'll find them:

🍁 **74**

🇺🇸 **264**

🇦🇺 **44**

The remaining **18** are scattered across the world

| | | |
|---|---|---|
| France | Japan | Thailand |
| Germany | Macedonia | UAE |
| Greece | New Zealand | UK |
| India | Spain | |

Australia has about 150 roadside attractions, but only 44 make it into the league of the world's largest.

• Sources: www.bigthings.com.au, www.roadsideamerica.com, www.wlra.us , www.wikipedia.org, www.bigtrip.com.au, www.biglucy.com.au/lucysbragginrights, and 'Big Things' by David Clark. Photograph: © S Kasprowicz

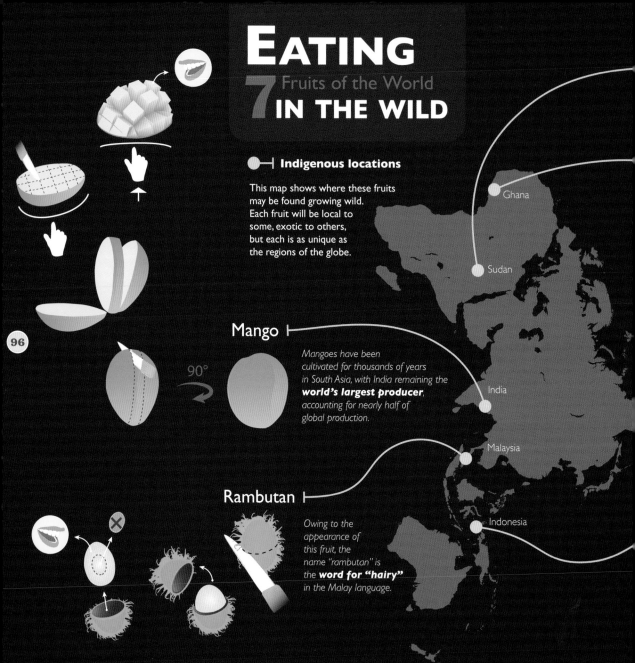

# EATING
## 7 Fruits of the World
# IN THE WILD

**○—┤ Indigenous locations**

This map shows where these fruits
may be found growing wild.
Each fruit will be local to
some, exotic to others,
but each is as unique as
the regions of the globe.

Ghana

Sudan

## Mango ┤

*Mangoes have been
cultivated for thousands of years
in South Asia, with India remaining the
**world's largest producer**,
accounting for nearly half of
global production.*

India

Malaysia

90°

## Rambutan ┤

*Owing to the
appearance of
this fruit, the
name "rambutan" is
the **word for "hairy"**
in the Malay language.*

Indonesia

**MAP SOURCE:** Eric Gaba (username Sting), Wikimedia Commons

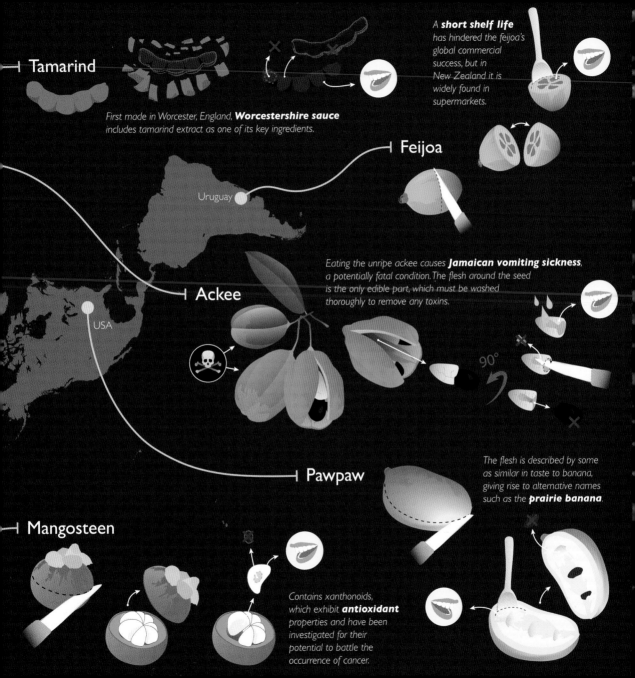

Tamarind

First made in Worcester, England, **Worcestershire sauce** includes tamarind extract as one of its key ingredients.

A **short shelf life** has hindered the feijoa's global commercial success, but in New Zealand it is widely found in supermarkets.

Feijoa

Uruguay

Eating the unripe ackee causes **Jamaican vomiting sickness**, a potentially fatal condition. The flesh around the seed is the only edible part, which must be washed thoroughly to remove any toxins.

Ackee

USA

90°

Pawpaw

The flesh is described by some as similar in taste to banana, giving rise to alternative names such as the **prairie banana**.

Mangosteen

Contains xanthonoids, which exhibit **antioxidant** properties and have been investigated for their potential to battle the occurrence of cancer.

# HIGHER GROUND

## 8 MUST-SEE VANISHING TOURIST DESTINATIONS

With global temperatures heating up and ocean levels on the rise, visit these endangered locations before they disappear forever (life preservers optional).

### 1 ▸ MT. KILIMANJARO, TANZANIA

Popular among seasoned climbing enthusiasts, the snowcaps of the highest mountain in Africa are melting at a torrid pace. It has already lost 85% of the snow its peaks adorned back in 1912, and the caps are projected to completely vanish by 2025.

### 4 ▸ SKI RESORTS, WORLDWIDE

Global temperatures are expected to rise 2°F (1.1°C) in the next 40 years, moving the snowbelt higher. This process will decimate popular lower-altitude resorts such as Whistler (Canada) and Kitzbühel (Austria). It is expected that 50% of all ski hills will be out of business by 2050.

### 2 ▸ GREAT BARRIER REEF, AUSTRALIA

Inhabited by 7150 different species, the reef is built by billions of tiny coral polyps, making it the world's largest structure constructed by living organisms. Vulnerable to coral bleaching, pollution and commercial shipping, the reef's coral could perish entirely as early as 2030.

### 3 ▸ VENICE, ITALY

Famous for its canals, Venice is now seriously threatened by water. Sinking 12" (30.5cm) in the past century, the city now averages more than 100 floods annually. Dangerous flooding levels are expected by 2050, so it's not a surprise that native Venetians will have fully emigrated by 2040.

# WATER WORLD - A GLIMPSE INTO THE FUTURE OF OUR OCEANS

Global sea levels are rising worldwide, albeit at different rates. This inconsistency is due to a multitude of factors, most notably the weight of the water, varying salinity contents and powerful underwater currents. The average annual increase in water is 0.62" (1.57cm). If this rate of elevation doesn't fluctuate, the oceans would rise a total of 54" (1.37m) by the end of this century. This would effectively change our existing coastlines and forcibly displace 10% of the human population.

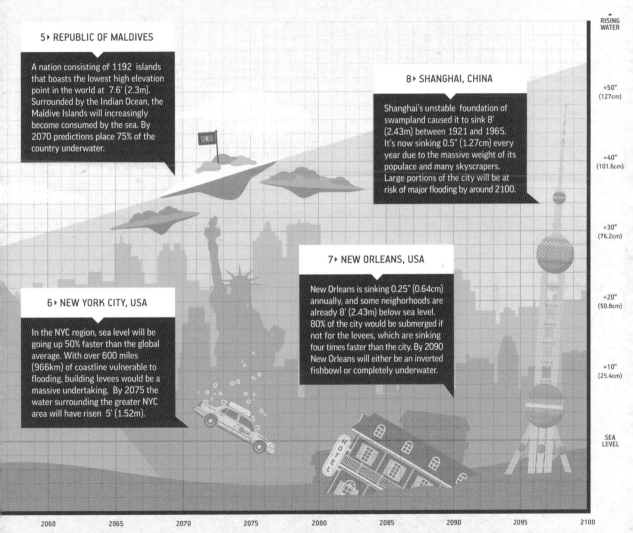

**RISING WATER**

## 5▸ REPUBLIC OF MALDIVES

A nation consisting of 1192 islands that boasts the lowest high elevation point in the world at 7.6' (2.3m). Surrounded by the Indian Ocean, the Maldive Islands will increasingly become consumed by the sea. By 2070 predictions place 75% of the country underwater.

## 8▸ SHANGHAI, CHINA

Shanghai's unstable foundation of swampland caused it to sink 8' (2.43m) between 1921 and 1965. It's now sinking 0.5" (1.27cm) every year due to the massive weight of its populace and many skyscrapers. Large portions of the city will be at risk of major flooding by around 2100.

## 7▸ NEW ORLEANS, USA

New Orleans is sinking 0.25" (0.64cm) annually, and some neighborhoods are already 8' (2.43m) below sea level. 80% of the city would be submerged if not for the levees, which are sinking four times faster than the city. By 2090 New Orleans will either be an inverted fishbowl or completely underwater.

## 6▸ NEW YORK CITY, USA

In the NYC region, sea level will be going up 50% faster than the global average. With over 600 miles (966km) of coastline vulnerable to flooding, building levees would be a massive undertaking. By 2075 the water surrounding the greater NYC area will have risen 5' (1.52m).

+50" (127cm)

+40" (101.6cm)

+30" (76.2cm)

+20" (50.8cm)

+10" (25.4cm)

SEA LEVEL

2060  2065  2070  2075  2080  2085  2090  2095  2100

SOURCES ▸ The Times Online, BBC, National Geographic, Guardian, Greenpeace, IPCC, MSNBC, Wikipedia, Yahoo, Reef & Rainforest Research Centre

# Two minutes of Tokyo.

One loop line, 29 stations, carrying millions of people each day, surrounding one of the world's largest city centres: the Yamanote Line in Tokyo.

You can get a continuous and dynamic perspective on Tokyo from a ride on the Yamanote Line. Here is a moment in Tokyo time from the window of a train.

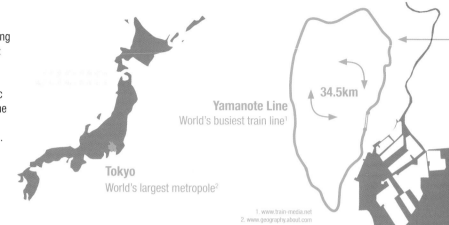

**Tokyo**
World's largest metropole[2]

**Yamanote Line**
World's busiest train line[1]

34.5km

1. www.train-media.net
2. www.geography.about.com

BUSINESS MAN

vending machine

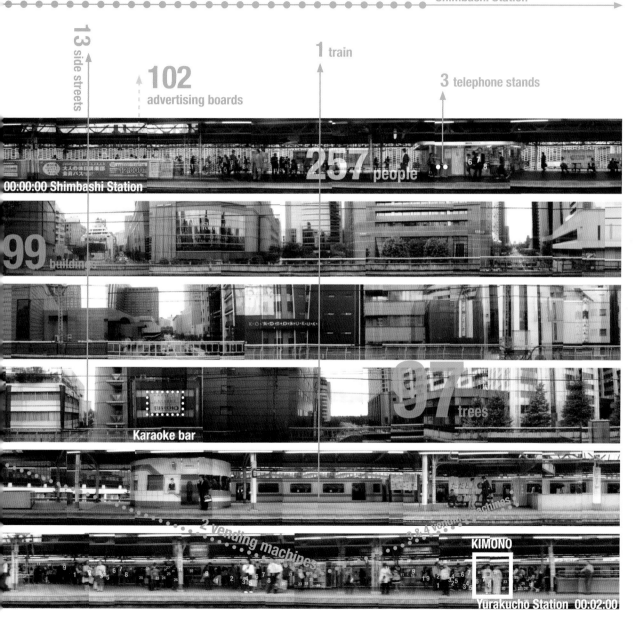

29 stations > 3,500,000 rides a day[1]

Shimbashi Station

13 side streets

102 advertising boards

1 train

3 telephone stands

257 people

00:00:00 Shimbashi Station

99 buildings

97 trees

Karaoke bar

2 vending machines

3 & 4 vending machines

KIMONO

Yūrakuchō Station 00:02:00

# Uluru

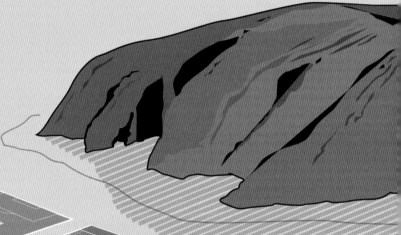

Australia

(Also known as Ayers Rock)

862.5m (2829ft) above sea level
348m (1141ft) high
3.6km (2.2 miles) long
1.9km (1.2 miles) wide
9.4km (5.8 miles) around the base
Covers 3.33 sq km (1.29 sq miles)

Covers the same surface area
as 462 international football
pitches (105m x 68m), or
612 American football
pitches (360ft x 160ft).

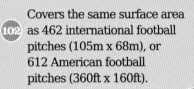

462

612

Research suggests that Indigenous Australians
have lived in the area for at least 10,000 years.

**10,000 BC**                                                    5,000 BC

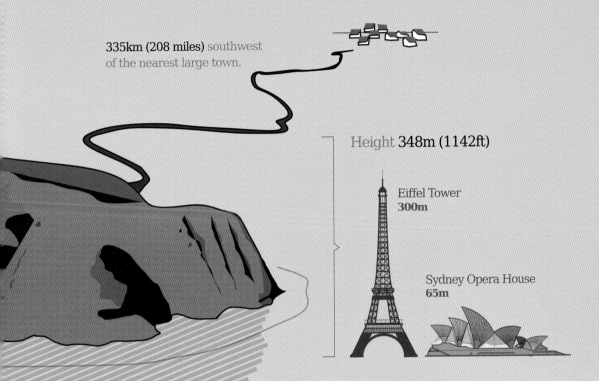

**335km (208 miles)** southwest of the nearest large town.

Height **348m (1142ft)**

Eiffel Tower
**300m**

Sydney Opera House
**65m**

Depth underground
**(unknown) 1000m +**

1995 - The park name was changed from Ayers Rock-Mount Olga National Park to Uluru-Kata Tjuta National Park, reflecting its traditional ownership and the Anangu people's close relationship with their land.

1985 - Title to the land was handed back to the traditional owners, the Anangu.

1873 - The first European to visit the rock, William Gosse, named it Ayers Rock after Sir Henry Ayers (the Chief Secretary of South Australia at the time).

1950 - Ayers Rock was made a national park.

1850

2011

AD

**Present day**

## Bikes Rule!
Cyclists Have Complete Right of Way

**19,000km**
The length of bicycle paths in the Netherlands (the most in the world)

**909km**
The average distance each Dutch person rides on their bicycle per year

## The Dutch Commute
Modes of travel by percentage

**16km/h**
Average bicycle speed

- bicycle
- walk
- car
- public transport
- other

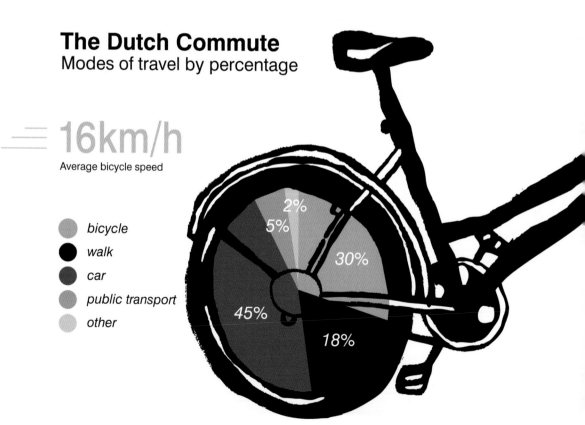

2%

5%

30%

45%

18%

# The Fit Dutch
Top 10 bike-riding countries: percentage of the population that cycle

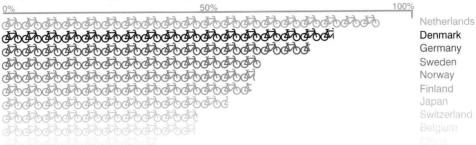

Netherlands
Denmark
Germany
Sweden
Norway
Finland
Japan
Switzerland
Belgium
China

## Heaps of Bikes
Sales of bicycles 2007

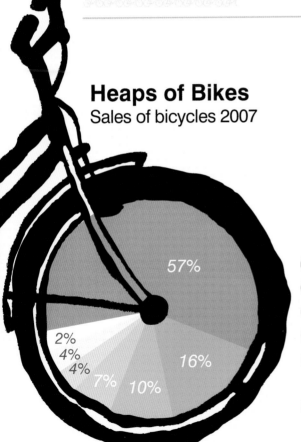

57%

2%
4%
4%
7%    10%    16%

**9.1% more bicycles than humans**

# 18,000,000

Population of bicycles in the Netherlands

# 16,400,000

Population of the Netherlands

- city bicycle
- child's bicycle
- trekking bicycle
- electric bicycle
- other
- mountain bicycle
- folding bicycle

www.nationmaster.com
www.rvz.net
www.holland.cyclingaroundtheworld.nl

# Talk to the hand

## The thumb and the forefinger

It may mean "two" in BELGIUM or the NETHERLANDS but flash this gesture in CHINA and people assume you're saying "eight". But avoid flashing it around in ITALY, as it means "not good".

## The "OK" sign

In most cultures it means "OK", but in some others it has a very different meaning. In VENEZUELA and TURKEY, for example, it means "homosexual". The BRAZILIANS see it as a vulgar insult, while in GERMANY it can either mean "OK" or an insult, depending on which part of the country you're in.

## The thumbs up

What means "all right" or "good" in the UK, SOUTH KOREA and SOUTH AFRICA carries a far different meaning in AFGHANISTAN, IRAN and IRAQ. If your travels ever bring you to those parts of the world, remember that the thumbs up is considered a vulgar insult. But in FRANCE or SWITZERLAND, it simply means "one".

They say that actions speak louder than words. But as far as hand gestures go, a simple action can also be more confusing than words. We take a look at what various hand gestures mean, depending on which part of the world you're in.

## The fingers brought together

Most commonly seen in ITALY as a gesture that asks "what's this?", but in other cultures it has various meanings, such as "little" (INDIA, CONGO), "beautiful" (TURKEY) and "wait a moment" (EGYPT).

# 86%

of communication lies in body language, and hands are considered an important part of nonverbal communication.

## The "come here" or "go away"

Another example of how a gesture can have one meaning in one culture and the direct opposite meaning in another. In the CZECH REPUBLIC, DENMARK and the NETHERLANDS, doing this means you're asking someone to go away. But in GHANA, PHILIPPINES and VIETNAM, it means you're asking someone to come to you.

Sources: Articlesbase (http://bit.ly/lqOpA9), The Guardian UK (http://bit.ly/irw2gc), www.aquiziam.com/gestures.html.

# TRAVELS IN TIME

**What if you could travel through time when you travel overseas?**

**5**
||||
This number is your approximate flight duration (not including the effects of wind) – that is, the number of hours you actually spend in the aeroplane.

**+12**
This number indicates how many hours after (+) or before (-) your departure time you'll arrive in your destination.

▼
This marker means that time will go backwards while you're in the aeroplane. You'll arrive at your destination in the past (before the time you left your point of departure).

▽
This marker means that time in the aeroplane will go faster than on the ground. You'll arrive in the future (but you'll have spent more hours in the aeroplane than will have passed on the ground).

▽
This marker means that time in the aeroplane will go slower than on the ground. You'll arrive in the future (but you'll have spent less hours in the aeroplane than will have passed on the ground).

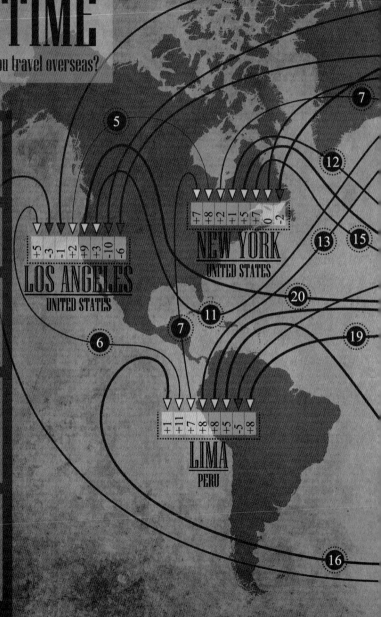

LOS ANGELES — UNITED STATES
+5 -3 -1 +2 +9 +3 -10 -6

NEW YORK — UNITED STATES
+7 +8 +2 +1 +5 +7 0 -2

LIMA — PERU
+1 +11 +7 +8 +8 +5 -5 +8

13  7  5  12  13  15  20  19  11  7  6  16

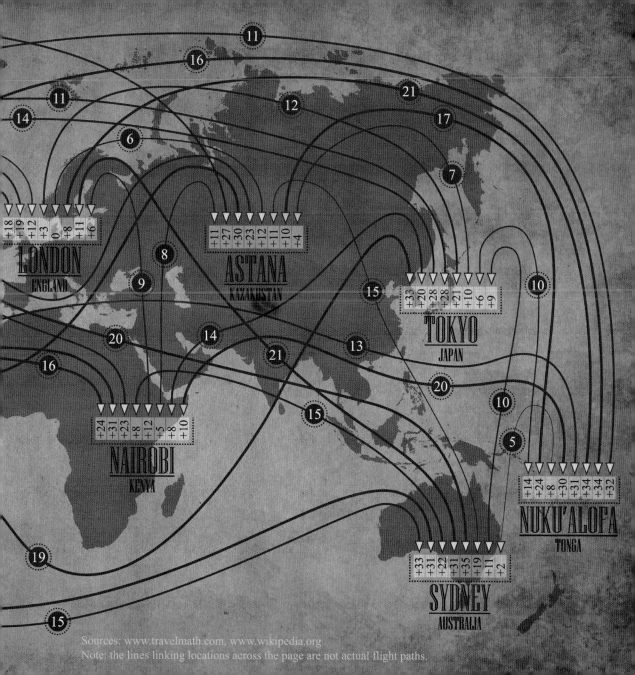

# Digitally Connected

Over the last 10 years, the number of websites devoted to travel has increased dramatically. Travellers are able to research and pre-book much of their travel, all in the comfort of their own home. With the advances in mobile device technology, travellers also have the ability to access an abundance of travel information on the road and stay in touch with their loved ones from almost every corner of the globe. This means that the availability of internet access is more important than ever for travellers

This infographic compares internet penetration rates – that is, how much of each country's population has access to the internet. And for travellers who like to take advantage of wi-fi (both free and paid-for), the number of wi-fi locations in each country (as at May 2010) appears in brackets.

**KEY**
- MIDDLE EAST
- AMERICAS
- EUROPE
- ASIA
- OCEANIA

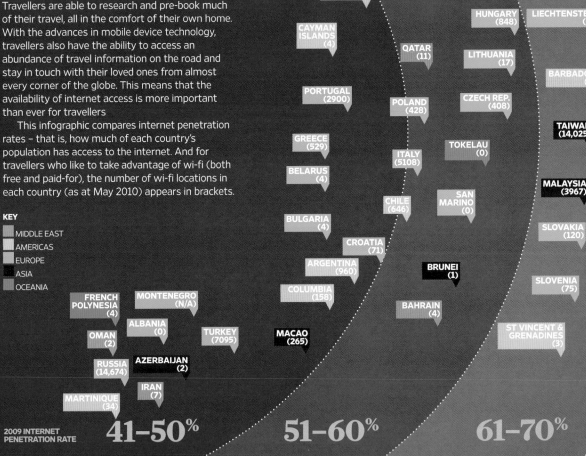

LATVIA (234)

NIUE (0)

JAMAICA (2)

MONA (

BARBADOS (3)

HUNGARY (848)

LIECHTENSTE (1

CAYMAN ISLANDS (4)

QATAR (11)

LITHUANIA (17)

BARBADO (

PORTUGAL (2900)

POLAND (428)

CZECH REP. (408)

TAIWAN (14,025)

GREECE (529)

ITALY (5108)

TOKELAU (0)

BELARUS (4)

MALAYSIA (3967)

CHILE (646)

SAN MARINO (0)

SLOVAKIA (120)

BULGARIA (4)

CROATIA (71)

BRUNEI (1)

SLOVENIA (75)

ARGENTINA (960)

COLUMBIA (158)

BAHRAIN (4)

ST VINCENT & GRENADINES (3)

FRENCH POLYNESIA (4)

MONTENEGRO (N/A)

ALBANIA (0)

OMAN (2)

TURKEY (7095)

MACAO (265)

RUSSIA (14,674)

AZERBAIJAN (2)

IRAN (7)

MARTINIQUE (34)

2009 INTERNET PENETRATION RATE

## 41–50%

## 51–60%

## 61–70%

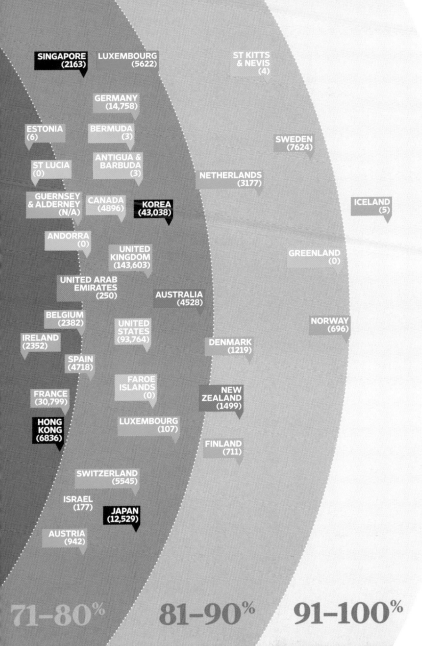

# Internet users

## 29%
OF THE WORLD'S
POPULATION HAS ACCESS
TO THE INTERNET

## 445%
GROWTH OF USERS
2000–2010

## 42%
OF USERS
ARE FROM ASIA

**COUNTRIES WITH
THE HIGHEST NUMBER
OF USERS IN 2010
(IN MILLIONS)**

1 CHINA (420.0)
2 UNITED STATES (239.9)
3 JAPAN (99.1)
4 INDIA (81.0)
5 BRAZIL (75.9)
6 GERMANY (65.1)
7 RUSSIA (59.7)
8 UNITED KINGDOM (51.4)
9 FRANCE (44.6)
10 NIGERIA (44.0)
11 SOUTH KOREA (39.4)
12 TURKEY (35.0)
13 IRAN (33.2)
14 MEXICO (30.6)
15 ITALY (30.0)
16 INDONESIA (30.0)
17 PHILIPPINES (29.7)
18 SPAIN (29.1)
19 ARGENTINA (26.6)
20 CANADA (26.2)

**SOURCES** INTERNETWORLDSTATS.COM,
V4.JIWIRE.COM/SEARCH-HOTSPOT-LOCATIONS.HTM

SINGAPORE (2163)
LUXEMBOURG (5622)
ST KITTS & NEVIS (4)
GERMANY (14,758)
ESTONIA (6)
BERMUDA (3)
SWEDEN (7624)
ST LUCIA (0)
ANTIGUA & BARBUDA (3)
NETHERLANDS (3177)
GUERNSEY & ALDERNEY (N/A)
CANADA (4896)
KOREA (43,038)
ICELAND (5)
ANDORRA (0)
UNITED KINGDOM (143,603)
GREENLAND (0)
UNITED ARAB EMIRATES (250)
AUSTRALIA (4528)
FALKLAND ISLANDS (0)
BELGIUM (2382)
UNITED STATES (93,764)
NORWAY (696)
IRELAND (2352)
DENMARK (1219)
SPAIN (4718)
FAROE ISLANDS (0)
NEW ZEALAND (1499)
FRANCE (30,799)
LUXEMBOURG (107)
HONG KONG (6836)
FINLAND (711)
SWITZERLAND (5545)
ISRAEL (177)
JAPAN (12,529)
AUSTRIA (942)

71–80%   81–90%   91–100%

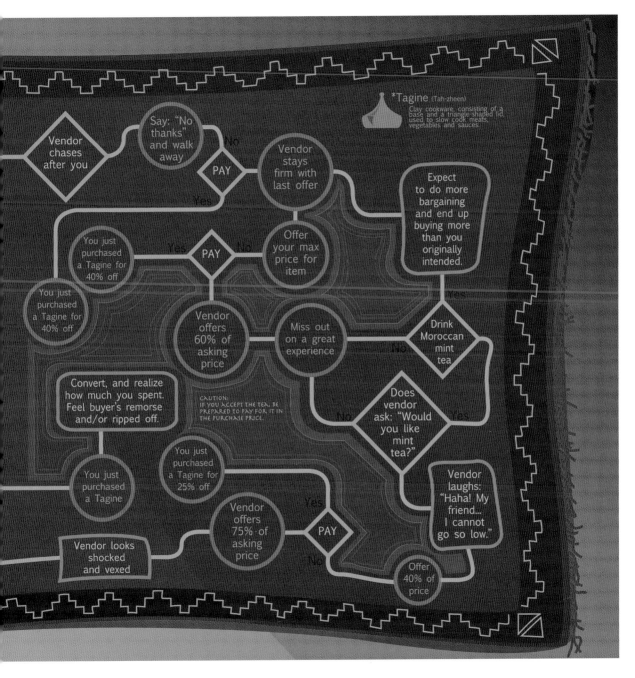

*Tagine (Tah-zheen)
Clay cookware, consisting of a base and a triangle-shaped lid, used to slow cook meats, vegetables and sauces.

Vendor chases after you

Say: "No thanks" and walk away

No

PAY

Vendor stays firm with last offer

Expect to do more bargaining and end up buying more than you originally intended.

Yes

You just purchased a Tagine for 40% off

Yes

PAY

No

Offer your max price for item

You just purchased a Tagine for 40% off

Vendor offers 60% of asking price

Miss out on a great experience

No

Drink Moroccan mint tea

Yes

Convert, and realize how much you spent. Feel buyer's remorse and/or ripped off.

CAUTION:
IF YOU ACCEPT THE TEA, BE PREPARED TO PAY FOR IT IN THE PURCHASE PRICE.

No

Does vendor ask: "Would you like mint tea?"

Yes

You just purchased a Tagine

You just purchased a Tagine for 25% off

Vendor laughs: "Haha! My friend... I cannot go so low."

Yes

Vendor looks shocked and vexed

Vendor offers 75% of asking price

PAY

No

Offer 40% of price

# Plugged in

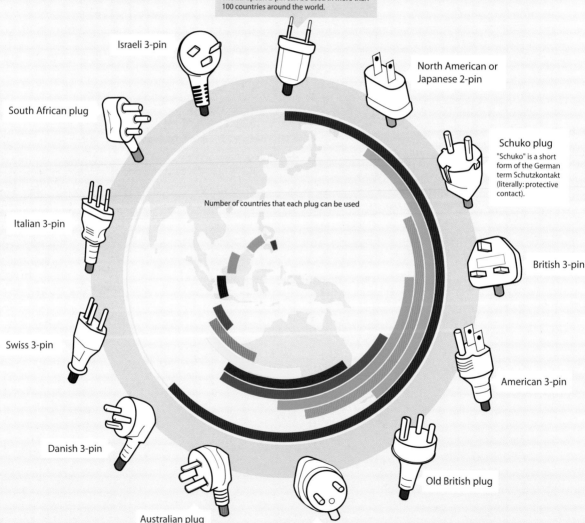

## European 2-pin
The European 2-pin can be used in more than 100 countries around the world.

Israeli 3-pin

South African plug

Italian 3-pin

Swiss 3-pin

Danish 3-pin

Australian plug

French 2-pin

North American or Japanese 2-pin

## Schuko plug
"Schuko" is a short form of the German term Schutzkontakt (literally: protective contact).

British 3-pin

American 3-pin

Old British plug

Number of countries that each plug can be used

114

## Central America

## Europe

## WEATHER

The climate is predominantly tropical. The average annual temperature is 28ºC in the north and 22ºC in the south.

**3.3%** is what tourism will contribute to Brazil's 2011 GDP.

## PORTUGUESE

Brazilian portuguese has an accent, intonation and grammar very different from what one hears in Portugal and other Portuguese former colonies.

# → Everything you need to know!

# Brazil

It's the fifth-largest country in the world and covers almost half of South America. Say hello to this friendly giant!

## NORTH

An ecotourism hot spot, hosting the largest, and most famous, tropical rainforest in the world – the Amazon.

**Regional tourism by the numbers...**

**2%** NORTH

**8%** NORTHEAST

**3%** CENTRAL WEST

**116**

**MANAUS Is the largest tourist destination in the Amazon.**

**WORTH THE TRIP** In addition to ecotourism, look out for Ver-o-Peso Market (Belém), the Da Paz Theatre (Belém) and the Amazonas Theatre (Manaus).

**58%** SOUTHEAST

**NATURAL BEAUTY** The region is famous for flora, fauna and its spectacular landscapes.

## CENTRAL WEST

This less populous region is home to the nation's capital. Flora and fauna are also good reasons to visit.

**BRASILIA Founded in 1960, the capital is a treat for fans of modernist architecture.**

**WORTH THE TRIP**
Don't miss the Pantanal wetlands in Mato Grosso and the tablelands around Guimaraes (Mato Grosso), and Veadeiros (Goias).

**29%** SOUTH

**Sources**: www.portalbrasil.net / http://www.braziltour.com / www.embratur.gov.br / **PHOTOS**: EMBRATUR

## Ten years of tourist arrivals in Brazil (millions)

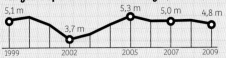

5,1 m — 1999
3,7 m — 2002
5,3 m — 2005
5,0 m — 2007
4,8 m — 2009

## CURRENCY

The Brazilian unit of currency is the Real (R$).

**97%** of tourists who visit Brazil say they would visit again.

## SOUTHEAST

The most economically-developed region of the country is also the most visited. A mix of urban experiences and natural world adventures can be enjoyed here.

Rio2016

**RIO DE JANEIRO** The city of Rio will host the Olympic Games in 2016 — the first time it will be held in South America.

**SÃO PAULO** A leader in urban tourism, São Paulo is well known for entertainment and gastronomy.

**WORTH THE TRIP** Minas Gerais and the historical cities of Ouro Preto, Mariana and Tiradentes; the beautiful beaches of Vitoria, capital of Espirito Santo; Rio de Janeiro's Carnival; São Paulo, the biggest city in Latin America.

## NORTHEAST

Think seaside towns and beautiful beaches! This is the target destination for most visitors to Brazil. As a result, tourism infrastructure is well-developed and makes for easy travel. Culture and ecotourism are also features for visitors to the region.

**SALVADOR** The original capital of the country, experience pristine beaches and colonial architecture.

## SOUTH

A strong European influence and the lowest temperatures of the country — a place to chill out.

**WORTH THE TRIP** spectacular Iguazu Falls in Paraná; the old-world charm of Joinville, Santa Catarina; and Florianópolis, well-known for its beautiful beaches.

**CURITIBA** This city is a little off the tourist trail, so it will be all yours. It has a multicultural heritage which informs its numerous parks, gardens and memorials.

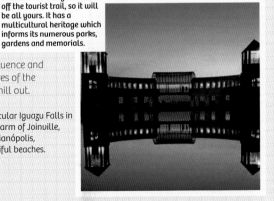

**MACEIÓ** Uniquely positioned between the Atlantic Ocean and the Mundaú Lake, this city is a must for beaches and water sports.

**WORTH THE TRIP** The region is home to the largest number of World Heritage Sites; the city of Olinda (Pernambuco); São Luís (Maranhão); and the historical center of Pelourinho, in Salvador (Bahia).

# A map giving every person living in the world the same amount of space

Each grid cell on the map is related to the same amount of space in the physical world. The size of a grid cell reflects the number of people living in that space in relation to the other grid cells. A grid cell twice as big as another has twice as much population.

Land Elevation
Metres

8000

0

## Data Sources
Global Topographic and Bathymetric Data: US Geological Survey (USGS)
Population Data: Center for International Earth Science Information Network (CIESIN), Columbia University; Centro Internacional de Agricultu

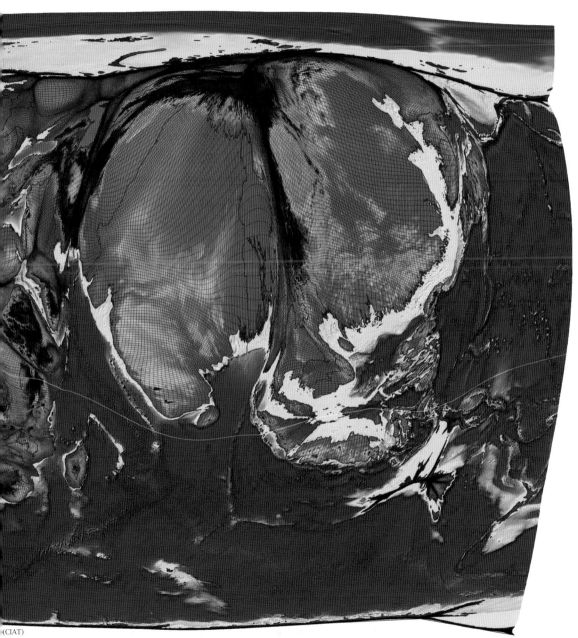

(CIAT)

# CONTRIBUTORS

## AMY MAYNARD

Amy Maynard is a young advertising and communications graduate and emerging freelance illustrator based in Brisbane, Australia.
www.amynmaynard.com

## ADRIAN KRONOWETTER

Crafting illustrative and informative designs, Land of Visions is the moniker for Montreal-based illustrator Adrian Kronowetter.
www.landofvisions.ca

## AMY MARTIN

Amy Martin is an interaction designer living and working in San Francisco, California.
www.amyemartin.com

## ANSELM BRADFORD

Anselm Bradford lectures in visual communication, interactive and web media as part of the Digital Media faculty at AUT University (Auckland, New Zealand). www.anselmbradford.com

**28**

**96**

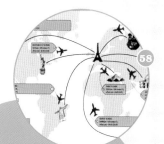

**40**

**52**

## BENJAMIN HENNIG

Benjamin Hennig is a passionate academic geographer. He was educated at the Universities of Cologne (Germany) and Sheffield (UK). Parts of his research are on display at www.viewsoftheworld.net.

**90**

**70**

**22**

**118**

**58**

## CAREN WEINER CAMPBELL

A magazine journalist turned data visualization consultant, Caren Weiner Campbell now runs her own information design firm, Synoptical Charts LLC, in Chapel Hill, North Carolina. www.synopticalcharts.com

## CHARLOTTE AUDREY OWEN-MEEHAN

Charlotte Audrey Owen-Meehan, is a freelance art director/illustrator, who also works in the field of motion graphics. She is currently based in Birmingham, UK. www.charlotteaudreyowenmeehan.com

**62**

# CONTRIBUTORS

## CONTINUED

## DAMIEN LERI

Damien Leri applies information technology to challenges in population health. His company is Big Yellow Star.
www.bigyellowstar.com

**86**

## CURTIS WHALEY

Tablet Infographics is the studio of Curtis Whaley and is located in Madison, Wisconsin.
www.tabletinfographics.com

## DAVID MOONEY

David Mooney is a graduate of Carleton University's Interactive Multimedia and Design program. David enjoys changing conceptual thoughts into tangible images through design, and he thanks Erin for all her help.
www.thrownshoe.ca

**112**

## CLARA HUI
## TINA KO

Clara Hui is an educational researcher. She loves writing, especially stories for children. She is also a sports addict who dreams of running all the marathons on her page! clarahui0908@gmail.com

Tina Ko is a freelance illustrator based in Hong Kong. She has published two books and draws for newspapers and businesses for years. She loves travelling a lot! tintinaa@gmail.com

## HANNAH BEATRICE

Hannah Beatrice is an illustrator and photographer based in Manchester, UK, with her roots lying in the Shetland Islands and her feet itching for travel further afield.
www.hannahbeatrice.co.uk

## IAN CHONG

Ian Chong is a designer from Australia who thinks the world can benefit from great information design. He loves travelling and couldn't believe a brief like this would come, ever!
www.ianchong.com

## FACTORIO.US

Factorio.us is a creative collective based in Milan and founded by three Italian designers: Andrea, Michele and Ruggero.
www.factorio.us

## JENIFER BULCOCK

Jenifer Bulcock is an Australian graphic designer based in Vancouver, Canada. She is currently working as a freelance designer for several international clients.
www.jeniferbulcock.com

# CONTRIBUTORS
## CONTINUED

## JESSICA PETER
## HEATHER PETER

Jessica Peter writes, travels, and researches. . . not necessarily in that order. You can find her blogging at www.jessicapeter.net

Heather Peter is a freelance graphic designer, and full-time marketing coordinator. Her portfolio is at www.heatherpeterportfolio .blogspot.com

80

*Cups of Tea* vs *Life Satisfac...*

## JENN DA COSTA

Jenn Da Costa is currently finishing her communication design degree at Swinburne University of Technology, Melbourne, Australia. She also works freelance.

14

104 9,000km
909km

HEELS

Heaps of Bikes

92

## KATYA CAMERON

Katya Cameron is new to information design and has just completed a final project at university focusing on it. She is currently gathering work experience in communication design in Melbourne before she picks up and moves to Amsterdam.

## KAITLIN YARNALL
## ÁLVARO VALIÑO

Kaitlin Yarnall is a trained cartographer and currently the deputy art director of the magazine *National Geographic*. She lives in Washington, DC.

Álvaro Valiño is an experienced designer, illustrator, and infographic artist. He is currently the graphics director for the Madrid-based newspaper, *Público*. www.alvarovalino.com

## LISA GOFF

Lisa Goff is an Australian-born graphic designer and illustrator based in London. Lisa finds inspiration in magazines, books, travelling, wandering and everyday life.
www.vangoffdesign.com

## MEGHANA KHANDEKAR

Meghana Khandekar is an artist and designer. Avid travel has influenced her to work on issues such as climate change, HIV/AIDS, community mapping and social organization.
www.mkhandekar.com

## LLOYD NEEL

Lloyd Neel is a recent graduate in graphic design and is currently working in the industry. He is located in a design firm just outside of London.
www.lloydneel.co.uk

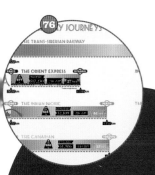

## MARK PEARSON

Mark Pearson's first love was putting ink on paper, then came DTP. His new passion is for delivering interesting information and insight graphically, with impact.
@mindfoundry

## MICHELLE KOH

Michelle Koh is a graduate communication designer from Melbourne's Swinburne University of Technology. She is currently residing in her home country, Singapore.

# CONTRIBUTORS
## CONTINUED

## PREETHI CHETHAN

Preethi Chethan is a designer from New York City and wants to use design to make the world better (oh, and loves information design). www.preethichethan.com

## NIGEL HOLMES

Nigel Holmes is a seasoned information designer and principal of Explanation Graphics, a design firm located just outside of New York City. www.nigelholmes.com

## RUBEN BERGAMBAGT

Ruben Bergambagt is an architect with a special interest in visualising urban complexity. He is currently practising in London and is a co-founder and owner of StudioNOA Architecture in Amsterdam. www.studionoa.eu

## PETER DUNCAN

Peter Duncan is a freelance graphic designer currently based in Oxford, UK. www.collectedpixels.co.uk

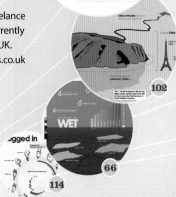

## SAMANTHA KASPROWICZ

Samantha Kasprowicz is a graphic designer and photographer who roams Sydney on her bike looking for new art, music and inspiration (and the elusive perfect cup of coffee). www.spikeandmambi.com

## PIERO ZAGAMI
## CARMEN VELA

Piero Zagami and Carmen Vela are two graphic designers from Italy and Spain. They both live and work in London.
www.pierozagami.com
www.carmenvela.com

## TIMOTHY CHAN
## LYDIA LIM

Lydia Lim is a senior art director at DDB Singapore, an advertising agency. Her work and background can be found at www.behance.net/leeds.

Timothy Chan is a senior copywriter at DDB Singapore, an advertising agency. His work and background can be found at www.behance.net/tim112.

## SANDY TAN

Sandy Tan is a freshly graduated communication designer from Swinburne University of Technology, Melbourne, Australia. She is currently residing in her home country, Singapore.

## TIAGO VELOSO
## FLÁVIA MARINHO

Tiago Veloso is a marketing and branding consultant, with a deep interest in data visualization. He's the creator of Visual Loop, one of the top places for infographics in the internet, featuring thousands of works from all over the world.

Flávia Marinho is a designer, living in São Paulo, with a vast experience in some of the most important media publications in that country, having won two SND awards, in 2009 and 2010.

## YEHONATAN KENAN

Yehonatan Kenan is a graphic designer, a graduate of Bezalel Academy of Arts and Design, lives and works in Jerusalem and loves infographics.
yonikenan@gmail.com

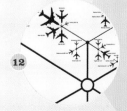

## HOW TO LAND A JUMBO JET

October 2011

## ACKNOWLEDGEMENTS

**Publisher** Piers Pickard

**Associate Publisher** Ben Handicott

**Cover Designers** Mark Adams, Kerrianne Southway

**Designers** James Hardy, Nic Lehman

**Layout** Kerrianne Southway, Mazzy Princep

**Editors** Asha Ioculari, Nigel Chin, Andrea Dobbin

**Print Production** Yvonne Kirk

Thanks also to Andrew Kean, Andy Kirk, David McCandless, Karl Gude

For the observant: US or UK spelling has been used in each infographic, depending on the background of the designer.

## PUBLISHED BY

Lonely Planet Publications Pty Ltd
ABN 36 005 607 983
90 Maribyrnong St, Footscray,
Victoria, 3011, Australia
www.lonelyplanet.com

10 9 8 7 6 5 4 3 2 1

Printed in China.

ISBN 978 1 74220 228 0

## LONELY PLANET OFFICES

**Australia**
Locked Bag 1, Footscray, Victoria 3011
Phone 03 8379 8000  Fax 03 8379 8111
Email talk2us@lonelyplanet.com.au

**USA**
150 Linden St, Oakland, CA 94607
Phone 510 250 6400  Toll free 800 275 8555
Fax 510 893 8572
Email info@lonelyplanet.com

**UK**
2nd Floor, 186 City Rd, London EC1V 2NT
Phone 020 7106 2100  Fax 020 7106 2101
Email go@lonelyplanet.co.uk

MIX
Paper from
responsible sources
FSC™ C021741
FSC
www.fsc.org